FAITH
THE SUPERNATURAL
CONNECTION

BY GREGG WEAR

Unless otherwise indicated, all Scripture quotations are taken from the *King James Version* of the Bible.

FAITH
THE SUPERNATURAL CONNECTION

Copyright 1999 by Gregg Wear
P.O. Box 1193
Sedalia, MO 65302

ISBN # 0-9671368-2-2

OTHER BOOKS BY GREGG WEAR

UNTANGLING THE HEALING CRISIS

HEALING ... We all want to be well and live a healthy, active lifestyle. Most of us have read or heard of various scriptures that mention healing. But...

* Is sickness good or is it bad?
* Is God glorified in sickness?
* What about Job?
* What about Paul's Thorn in the flesh?
* One good, sincere Christian who believed God would heal their disease, later died of that disease...Why?
* Over the years some people have been prayed for countless times, yet they are still sick...Why?
* What does the Bible say about doctors and medicine?
* I had a minister pray for my healing. Is it wrong for me to take my medicine?

THESE QUESTIONS PLUS MORE ARE ALL ANSWERED IN THIS BOOK ON DIVINE HEALING. Not only are these plaguing questions answered, but this, too, is written in plain, simple terms to forever settle any doubt in your mind that GOD WANTS YOU HEALED AND HEALTHY.

In addition, this 206 page book teaches you HOW to receive the healing God has provided. The price is $10.00, plus $2.00 for shipping and handling.

Gregg Wear Ministries
P.O. Box 2341
Lees Summit, MO 64082

PIECING TOGETHER THE PROSPERITY PUZZLE

PROSPERITY...We all want to be successful and enjoy a prosperous life. We all want to be better off today than we were yesterday, and better off tomorrow than we are today. But...

* Does God want us to prosper financially?
* Is money evil?
* What about the rich, young ruler?
* What about Jesus?
* Are there any Bible characters that were both godly and wealthy?
* How does financial prosperity come from God?
* What role do tithes and offerings play in our prosperity?
* What is the ultimate purpose of experiencing financial prosperity?

THESE QUESTIONS PLUS MORE ARE ALL ANSWERED IN THIS BOOK. This book, too, is written in plain, simple terms to forever settle any doubt in the reader's mind that GOD WANTS YOU TO PROSPER FINANCIALLY.

In addition, this 201 page book teaches you HOW to allow God to bless and increase your finances. The price is $10.00, plus $2.00 for shipping and handling.

To order, write:

Gregg Wear Ministries
P.O. Box 2341
Lees Summit, MO 64082

TABLE OF CONTENTS

SECTION 1 — BELIEVING

SECTION 2 — SPEAKING

SECTION 3 — STANDING

- Table of Contents continued next page

FAITH
THE SUPERNATURAL
CONNECTION

SECTION 1
BELIEVING

Introduction

Who through faith...obtained promises,
- Hebrews 11:33

It would be meaningless to have a book on the subject of faith without having a clear understanding from the beginning of faith's key ingredient — believing. The only reason that faith has seemed so mysterious and confusing to so many people is because of a lack of a simple definition.

Many people unwittingly use the word "believe" as an erroneous substitute for other words or phrases. Instead of saying, *"I suppose so,"* they say, *"I believe so."* Instead of saying, *"I'm not sure about the answer,"* they say, *"I believe that is the answer."* Instead of saying, *"I'm surprised at the outcome,"* they say, *"I can't believe it."*

This is why they're confused when they read the word "believe" in the Bible. To them, believing is supposing, or something they're unsure of, or a surprise. Unfortunately, if you call a Tiger a dog long enough some people will start thinking that a Tiger is a dog. If you send the kids outside to play with the pet "dog" that you brought home from the exotic pet store, sooner or later you're going to have a problem.

Because people use the word "believe" to mean something other than what the Biblical use is, when they read "believe" in their Bible they're not cognizant of what they're truly reading. Therefore, section 1 will be devoted to examining the word "believe." Once this word is understood the rest on the subject of faith should fall into place.

What Things Can We Ask For?

Secondly, what can we use our faith to receive? Some people are looking to receive some rather outrageous things. For example, does a person have a right to ask God to make them the first astronaut to go on a manned space flight to the planet of Mars? Can people ask God to alter their genetic makeup so that they can grow blonde hair instead of brown hair? Can people ask God to give them comic-book-super-powers such as flying, x-ray vision, and increased strength so that they can be world heroes?

These questions may sound outrageously silly to the majority of us, but I've observed that there's sometimes a very small minority that will vie for such answers. When such things don't come to pass, they become very vocal and end up causing a reproach to the subject of faith and the cause of Christ.

Believing

So, what things can we ask God for? The answer is really quite simple. Hebrews 11:33 is as definitive as can be.

Who through faith...OBTAINED PROMISES...
- Hebrews 11:33

We can use our faith to receive any of the hundreds of promises that God has given us in His Word. Why should we waste time focusing on things other than what the Bible is offering? The promises are so incredulous in themselves that it's foolish to get caught up even thinking about comic-book-super-powers, or whatever.

Think about what God is offering. For sickness, God is offering healing. For poverty, God is offering prosperity. For danger, God is offering protection. If we lack wisdom, He's promised to give it to us. If we need direction, we have His assurance He'll lead us. If fact, because of what God has promised, we need not have any fear of harm, disaster, incurable disease, financial difficulty, nor worldly and demonic forces. Should something bad somehow slip in through the back door of our lives, for any disaster God is offering restoration and the miraculous.

How The Promises Are Obtained

Notice this scripture again:

Who THROUGH FAITH...obtained promises...
- Hebrews 11:33

This is the key to receiving the promises of God —

9

through faith. They're not received by having a perfect church attendance for 50 years, nor are they received by joining a church. They're not received by being sincere people, and neither are they received by doing good works. *The promises of God are obtained through faith!*

Of course, we should want to be sincere, we should want to do good works, and we need to attend church. Yet as wonderful as all these are, they're not God's method for receiving what He has promised.

If we could obtain the promises of God by being a Sunday School teacher, then how would the person who was not a Sunday School teacher receive them? If we could obtain them by cooking meals for the needy, then how would the business-man, who has to work many hours a day and doesn't have the time to cook for the needy, receive the promises? If we could obtain the promises by sending thousands of dollars to missionaries, then how would a 14 year old young person, who cannot yet send thousands of dollars, receive?

Every person has a specific role in this life that they are to fulfill. Some cook meals in the church, some teach Sunday School, and some are called to teach and preach in the pulpit. Whatever our role, we are to fulfill that God-given call. *But that God-given call does not put one in the front of the line to receive the promises of God more quickly than any other God-given call.*

No Short-Cuts Or Favorites

Some people think that they have a short-cut to God

because they teach Sunday School. Others think that they have a short-cut to God because they're in a pulpit ministry. Others yet think that they're favorites because they don't sin as much as someone else. Again, our "works" are not the basis for receiving the promises of God.

Of course, we thank God for the Sunday School teachers, we thank God for all the preachers, and we thank God for those who cook meals in the church. *But there is not any particular calling that is more advantageous to receiving the promises of God.*

If we teach, we do so because God has equipped us to teach. If we preach, we do so because God has equipped us to preach. If we cook, we do so because God has blessed us with that particular ability. Our calling is a God-ordained call that simply means we are supposed to be doing something other than what someone else is called to do. When everyone is doing what they're supposed to do, more and more people in the world will come to know God and be blessed by the Church.

Thus, because of the many different callings God has set in the Church, God has made the promises available to every person through the *same* link, *the link of faith*. The pastor receives the promises just like the businessman. The Sunday School teacher receives the promises just like one who cooks meals for the needy. The elderly receives the promises just like the young. *We all receive the promises of God through faith!!*

Sadly, many have never understood this. I've heard people

say, *"I don't understand why God didn't answer their prayer. They were a preacher."* Others have said, *"Why didn't God heal that lady? She's the hardest worker this church has ever seen."* Some have said, *"If sister so-and-so can't receive I certainly won't receive, because she does more good works than I."*

But again, what these people have failed to realize is that God doesn't fulfill His promises in our lives because of good things that we do, or because we may be called to preach. God fulfills His promises to those people who receive *through faith*. Faith is the hand that receives from the hand of God.

God wants everyone to be blessed spiritually, financially, mentally, and physically. This is God's greatest desire. He wants us to prosper and be in health even as our souls prosper (3 John, verse 2). There are no favorites with God, because the truth is, we're all special to God (Acts 10:34). We all receive from God on the same basis — faith.

This is why it's absolutely imperative for all of us to *learn* how to receive from God. Our individual callings don't do it, and neither do our good works. Faith is the key that unlocks all of heaven's treasures. The person who learns to use his faith is a person who will be greatly blessed of God.

The Purpose Of This Book

The purpose of this book is to make available to the reader how the promises of God are received. If we haven't received we need to know why. We also need to know what we need to implement or change in order to receive. As Hosea 4:6

states, *"My people are destroyed for a lack of knowledge."* Thus, a thorough working knowledge on the subject of faith is what will produce results. A good rule of thumb to follow based on this scripture is — if we're still being destroyed, more information is needed.

Faith is not difficult, it just has to be learned. If you'll take the time to get instruction and practice, like anything else such as driving a car or typing on a typewriter, you can do it. *How proficient you become is up to you.* Many times we're only missing one small ingredient that can spark our understanding to make the difference in releasing our faith. Your life can make a tremendous impact on those around you. The world is looking for answers. Before you can be the greatest blessing to others, you must first be blessed. Jesus said, *"Occupy till I come."* So until He comes again, let's get about the business of occupying the way God meant us to occupy. Our faith is the victory that overcomes the world (1 John 5:4).

CHAPTER 1

WHAT IT MEANS TO BELIEVE

And all things, whatsoever ye shall ask in prayer, BELIEVING, ye shall receive.

- Matthew 21:22

What things soever ye desire, when ye pray, BELIEVE that ye receive them, and ye shall have them.

- Mark 11:24

To receive something from God, there's more involved than prayer alone. For example, Matthew 21:22 does not read, "and all things whatsoever ye shall ask in prayer, ye shall receive." Neither does Mark 11:24 read, "What things soever ye desire, pray, and ye shall have them." If this were the case, everyone all over the world would get their prayers answered. Obviously, though, this isn't so.

The key to answered prayer is in the word "believe." It says, *"**believe** that ye receive them."* Because many people have not had an understanding of this word their prayer lives have been hindered. It's a shame, really, that a simple definition of terms should have affected so many prayers.

So what does it mean to believe? According to the *Webster's Revised Unabridged Dictionary* (1913), the definition of "believe" is, *"to accept as true."* Then notice the word "as" in this definition — *"to accept as true."* The definition of "as" is, *"denoting equality."* In other words, there's not any *physical* proof that what we are accepting to be true *is* true, but we are accepting it *as* being true. Thus, by putting these two parts together the definition of believe would be:

To accept something as being true without any physical proof.
- definition of believe

By substituting this definition in the place of believe, Mark 11:24 and Matthew 21:22 would read as follows:

What things soever ye desire, when ye pray, accept it as being true without any physical proof that ye receive them, and ye shall have them.

And all things, whatsoever ye shall ask in prayer, accepting it as being true without any physical proof, ye shall receive.

As can plainly be seen, we first must accept it as being true without any physical proof that our prayer has been answered before we can physically have it. If we're praying for healing, we must first accept it as being true without any physical

16

proof that we're healed, then we'll be healed. If we're praying for financial needs to be met, we must first accept it as being true without any physical proof that our financial needs are met, then they'll be met.

This is the kind of faith that, according to Hebrews 11:6, pleases God. It honors God when we accept His Word as being true over what we can physically see or feel. We believe our prayer is answered simply because Jesus told us to believe that our prayer is answered. When we believe it is so, our answer will then come to pass. This is the difference between *believing* and *knowing.*

Believing And Knowing Are Not The Same

Knowing has to do with what can be seen or felt. Believing has to do with what's not seen or felt. The definition of "know" is, *"a __conscious__ awareness of the truth or facts."* In other words, knowing has to do with facts and truth from a _conscious_ standpoint. Believing has to do with facts and truth from a _trusting_ standpoint.

Jesus is not saying, "when you pray, _know_ that you receive them." If this were the case, you would immediately see or feel the answer to your prayer. You would have a conscious awareness that it was so. If your prayer was to be healed, you would immediately *feel* healed, that is, you would _know_ you were healed.

But contrary to knowing, Jesus said, "when you pray, _believe_ that you receive them." This means that God wants us to take a step of faith by _trusting_ that our prayer is answered.

17

He wants us to bypass what we can see or feel from a conscious standpoint and accept our answer as being true from a trusting standpoint. We *believe* that our prayer is answered.

Because some have not understood the difference between believing and knowing, people have unwittingly made erroneous statements. They've said, *"When I feel better I'll believe I'm healed."* The truth is, when they feel better they'll *know* they're healed. It's when they don't feel better that they must *believe* they're healed.

Yet people are continually checking their bodies to see if their prayer was answered. If they don't feel any better, or if they don't see a change in their body, they don't think that their prayer was answered. This is contrary to the nature of faith. They're unconsciously reverting to the thinking of when-I-feel-better-I'll-believe-I'm-healed mentality.

Again, Jesus said, *"when you pray, **believe** that you receive them."* We must believe that we've obtained our answer in spite of what we see or feel. In other words, using healing as an example, even though we don't feel any better or look any different after prayer, we nonetheless believe that we're healed. What follows after the believing is the having.

...believe that ye receive them, and ye shall have them.

We first *believe* that we're healed, then we'll *have* our healing. To wait until we have our healing before we believe that we're healed is backward to what Jesus said. Certainly the goal of every prayer is to have our desire, but the having will only come after the believing.

I realize that this is contrary to human reasoning, but human reasoning also says there isn't a heaven or a hell, nor a God in heaven. Human reasoning is finite and is limited to microscopes and telescopes. So if human reasoning is wrong about heaven, hell, and God, why should we think it's correct about how prayers are answered?

We need to learn to rely on what *Jesus* said about how prayers are answered. Since Jesus said to *believe* that our prayer is answered before we *have* our answer, we must rely on what He said on the subject of faith.

The scriptural order to answered prayer is simple — 1) have a desire, 2) pray, 3) believe that we receive them, and 4) have it. The only reason prayer has seemed difficult to some is because of their misunderstanding of what it means to believe. To believe that we receive something means that we accept the answer as being true without any physical proof. We move into the realm of trusting.

CHAPTER
2

THE FIG TREE PRECEDENT

And in the morning, as they passed by, they saw the fig tree dried up from the roots. And Peter calling to remembrance saith unto him, Master, behold the fig tree which thou cursedst is withered away.

- Mark 11:20-21

To wait until we _know_ that our prayer is answered before we _believe_ that our prayer is answered is backward to the scriptural precedent. We first believe it to be so, then we know it to be so.

In the eleventh chapter of the gospel of Mark we see the difference between believing and knowing. Jesus reveals the workings of faith, first by _demonstration_ and then by _explanation._ We see him first use his faith on an unproductive fig

21

tree, then we see the answer come to pass by the following day, and then he teaches us about all that took place. All of the key elements that God considers most important about faith are found in this account — a precedent.

Day 1

And on the morrow, when they were come from Bethany, he was hungry: And seeing a fig tree afar off having leaves, he came, if haply he might find any thing thereon: and when he came to it, he found nothing but leaves; for the time of figs was not yet.
- Mark 11:12-13

As Jesus was going into Jerusalem one particular morning he saw a fig tree in the distance. Noticing that the tree had grown its leaves he assumed that the tree should have its fruit. (One characteristic of the fig tree is that it produces its fruit before it produces its leaves — *Illustrated Davis Dictionary of the Bible*, pg. 243). When Jesus arrived at the tree it didn't have any fruit. Since the tree was an unproductive tree Jesus seized this moment as an opportunity to teach his disciples about the power of faith. So he cursed the tree:

And Jesus answered and said unto it, No man eat fruit of thee hereafter for ever. _And his disciples heard it._
- Mark 11:14

This is very important. After Jesus cursed the fig tree, you notice that the disciples did not _see_ any change in the tree. They only _heard_ what Jesus said to the tree. Based on the proper definitions of the words "believe" and "know," the dis-

22

ciples didn't _know_ that the fig tree was dead at this point. After all, they didn't _see_ anything different about the tree. The fig tree appeared to look just the same after Jesus had spoken to it as it did before Jesus had spoken to it. To _know_ that the fig tree was dead would require evidence other than what could be seen with the eye. Jesus, technically speaking, didn't _know_ that the tree was dead, he _believed_ that the tree was dead. Until we can see, we have to believe.

Day 2

And in the morning, as they passed by, they saw the fig tree dried up from the roots. And Peter calling to remembrance saith unto him, Master, behold, the fig tree which thou cursedst is withered away.
- Mark 11:20-21

The next morning as Jesus was going back into Jerusalem they passed by the fig tree He had cursed the preceding morning. When the disciples saw that the tree was withered away, Peter exclaimed, *"Master, look at the fig tree you cursed yesterday. It's withered away."*

At this point it can be _seen_ that the fig tree is dead. There's no doubt about it now, the disciples _know_ that the fig tree is dead. It's shrunken and withered, and all signs of life are long gone. There's nothing that has to be _believed_ now, it's _known_ that the tree is dead.

Again, we see that believing comes before knowing. Knowing doesn't cause believing, believing causes knowing. We don't know it to be so and then believe it. We believe it to be so, and then know it. We also see that the fig tree dried up from the roots:

> **And in the morning, as they passed by, they saw the fig tree dried up *from the roots.***
>
> **- Mark 11:20**

Here is our confirmation that when Jesus cursed the fig tree it truly died, even though it couldn't be seen to be dead in verse 14. The tree died underneath the ground where the life of that tree was — in the roots. Yet above the ground, the tree *appeared* to be just as much alive as it did before Jesus had said anything to it. The leaves were just as green, the trunk just as sturdy, yet, *where the eye couldn't see, it had died.*

This is important — appearances can be deceiving. The very moment that Jesus released his faith by speaking to the fig tree, the tree was dead, even though at the moment it appeared to be anything but dead. Yet, from that moment forward, it was now just a matter of time before the tree began to wither away.

This is one reason why we shouldn't be disappointed if or when events in our lives don't look different after prayer. The person praying in faith is never moved by above-the-ground information, only by underneath-the-ground information. Actually, to be disappointed because circumstances haven't changed after prayer is to unconsciously want to *know* that prayer was answered rather than to *believe* that prayer was answered.

Believing is what pleases God, not knowing. Hebrews 11:6

plainly states, *"...without faith it is impossible to please God...".* If we'll simply learn to be patient and believe, we'll be able to see the results of our faith. By Jesus believing that the tree was dead when he spoke, the outcome of the tree was later seen by the disciples. The tree was just as dead on Day 1 as it was on Day 2, but it took the 24 hours before it could be seen to be dead.

The Explanation

And Jesus answering saith unto them, Have faith in God. For verily I say unto you, That whosoever shall say unto this mountain, Be thou removed, and be thou cast into the sea; and shall not doubt in his heart, but shall believe that those things which he saith shall come to pass; he shall have whatsoever he saith. Therefore I say unto you, What things soever ye desire, when ye pray, believe that ye receive them, and ye shall have them.

- Mark 11:22-24

Jesus is now answering the question which must have been evident on the faces of the disciples, *"How could this be?"* The reason, Jesus explained, was by having faith in God. In fact, Jesus said that *anyone* could do what he just did.

"...I say unto you, That _WHOSOEVER_ shall say unto this mountain..."

- Mark 11:23

In other words, this ability to have faith is not limited only to pulpit-type ministries, such as the apostle, prophet, evangelist, pastor or teacher as listed in Ephesians 4:11. This same faith is available to any believer, great or small, young or old, who will simply apply it. Really, this is a rather remarkable statement made by Jesus. From the human standpoint, it's so easy to think that only well-known religious leaders can have faith like this. But as we move over into the New Testament Church, the apostle Paul said, *"God has dealt to **EVERY PERSON** the measure of faith"* (Romans 12:3). The only reason it hasn't been used is simply because it hasn't been taught.

What dynamic, well-known pulpiteers are accomplishing in their ministries with the masses should serve as an example of what the individual Christian can accomplish in his or her own life on a personal basis. Jesus plainly stated that *anyone* could not only do what he did with the fig tree, but if necessary, they could even move mountains. Whosoever means anyone and everyone.

Saying Is Important To Faith

Also, faith is composed not only of believing, but speaking. If we believe, it makes sense that we should speak. To not speak if we believe is unnatural and illogical. We follow through with our beliefs by speaking. According to v.23, we are to *"believe that those things which we **say** shall come to pass."* The person who hesitates to say what he believes is really exposing his lack of belief. Speaking should be an expression of what's in our heart. To speak something different than what we believe will ultimately bring confusion to our spirit. Our words should be in complete agreement with our hearts. Without the speaking of words a belief in the heart won't come to pass.

...Have _faith_ in God. For verily I say unto you, That whosoever shall _say_...

If a person wants to receive something from God with their faith they must _say_ something. If they refuse to speak their faith, or if they're not aware that they must speak their faith, their faith won't produce that which they desire. A belief in the heart must be released through the mouth.

CHAPTER
3

MARK 11:24

Therefore I say unto you, What things soever ye desire, when ye pray, believe that ye receive them, and ye shall have them.

- Mark 11:24

To help simplify this statement made by Jesus I've divided this verse into three parts:

1) What things so ever ye desire,
2) when ye pray, believe that ye receive them,
3) and ye shall have them.

I want to examine each part individually, on its own. Once we have an understanding of each part we can then put this verse together again.

1) What things so ever ye desire...

This is the purpose for praying the prayer of faith — *to receive something that we need or desire*. God is concerned about meeting our every need, and He is concerned about fulfilling the desires of our heart. God has given us more than enough promises to fulfill all that we could need or desire. In short, God has given us a blank check for all that He has in His bank account, so to speak. *If we can find what we need or want in his Word, it's ours for the asking.*

To receive something from God, whether it's healing, financial, or one of the many promises, we must be definite about what it is we want. According to the dictionary, the definition for the word "desire" means, *"to long for intensely."* Another similar definition says, *"an intense longing."*

I think many times we have overlooked the meaning of this word "desire." Or maybe I should say that we haven't read into it what I think Jesus was really trying to get across. Whatever it is that we want from God, it has to be something that we long for *intensely*. It must be something we *strongly* want and long for.

An excellent example of this is found with the woman with the issue of blood in Mark chapter 5. It states in verse 26 that she had suffered *many* things of *many* physicians. Of course, it's bad enough to suffer just *one* thing of *one* physician, but she evidently must have suffered much, because it doesn't say that she suffered a *few* things of a *few* physicians. So obviously she was willing to do *anything* and go see *anyone* if there was the remotest possibility that she could get well. *She wanted to be healed more than she wanted anything in this world.*

This is the kind of desire, that inward drive, that separates those who receive from God and those who don't. To receive something from God, that "thing," whatever it is, must be something that we long for *intensely*.

Further Examples Of Desire

Recall the different individual cases of healing in the ministry of Jesus. Examine the accounts of Jairus, the ruler of the synagogue in Mark chapter 5, the man with the palsy in Luke chapter 5, the woman of Canaan in Matthew chapter 15, the father of the demonized son in Mark chapter 9, and Blind Bartimeus in Mark chapter 10. What is the link, besides their faith, that is common in each of these accounts? *The answer is that these people longed intensely for a miracle.* They overcame incredible obstacles to be able to get what they so desperately needed.

For example, Jairus was willing to give up his professional career, for he could have been excommunicated and disgraced. The man with the palsy had to have his friends destroy another man's roof, which would have been a considerable expense to someone in his condition. The woman of Canaan faced apparent racism and rejection. The father of the demonized son faced despair and failure when the Lord's disciples failed to deliver his son. Blind Bartimeus faced a whole multitude unwilling to help him get to Jesus, and even tried to hush him up.

Desire Is Not A Preference

A preference is not a desire. Clearly, many people do not *desire* to be healed, they only *prefer* to be healed. In other words, they *prefer* healing over sickness, but they don't possess enough of a strong inward drive to motivate them to doing whatever it takes to get their healing.

Certainly most people prefer healing over sickness. They prefer prosperity over indebtedness. *But faith doesn't work on preferences, faith works on desires.* I think one reason many people never get any answers to their prayers is because they're not telling God what they desire, only what they prefer.

I've observed that if people have the ability to get along without what they need, they rarely exert the needed energy to do what's necessary to possess the promise. Like the children of Israel, some have learned to just "get by" in the wilderness of life, so to speak, and they have no desire to exert any energy to enter the promised land. They would *prefer* to be in the promised land, but they don't want to do what it takes to *possess* the promised land.

Sometimes a desire has to be cultivated. It may start as a whim, later grow into a preference, and eventually develop into a true desire. Sometimes it's necessary to examine us to find out what we *really* want, what we *truly* desire. Sometimes all we need to make is a 10 second adjustment in our spirit. We don't have to wait until our back is against the wall before we know what it is that we want. Regardless, it's important to know what it is that we want.

These Bible characters just mentioned were people who knew what they wanted. They had definitely pinpointed their desires. There wasn't a shadow of a doubt in their minds about what they wanted. This is the kind of a desire that Jesus is talking about in Mark 11:24. Like those who had received their healing in the four gospels, we have to pinpoint our desire. We should no longer *half-heartedly* want something. We shouldn't just simply *prefer* a blessing. *We must truly desire, above all things, that particular want or need.* We must isolate what it is that we want so that we can be definite about it when we pray.

2) ...when ye pray, believe that ye receive them...

This part of the verse sets the time that we lay hold by faith on whatever it is that we desire. You see, God wants to answer prayers and to meet needs and fulfill desires, but God has put the responsibility on *our* shoulders to make the first move. Jesus said, *"...your Father knoweth what things ye have need of, **before ye ask him**"* (Matthew 6:8).

This is an important truth to realize. Many people have the mistaken idea that because God knows what they have need of, they assume that God will meet their need, sooner or later, in the appropriate time. This is incorrect. According to Jesus, *we still have to ask God* in order for God to meet our need. Again, it is our responsibility to recognize our own need or desire and to respond in the correct procedure that God has ordained — *by asking in faith.*

According to Jesus we are to believe that we receive our desires *when we pray.* Jesus clearly said, *"when you pray, believe that you receive them."* You notice that he didn't say, *"after 30 minutes has elapsed, believe that you receive them,"* or, *"when a calendar month has expired, believe that you receive them. "*

Instead, Jesus is *very precise* about the moment we are to believe that we receive them. We're not waiting on God to set the time. *God is waiting on us to set the time.* It's important to realize that God has already answered "yes" to His promises and He's waiting for us to do something about them. His time is when *we* set the time.

When it comes to the promises that God has given us in His Word, the will of God is the Word of God. The two go hand-in-hand. 2 Corinthians 1:20 states, *"all the promises of God are yea, and in him amen."* In other words, God has already responded with a "yes" to any and every promise that is in the Word of God, the Bible.

For us to receive, it is now simply a matter of us laying hold on what God is already offering. How do we do this? The answer is by *us* setting a time to "believe that we receive them." According to Jesus here in Mark 11:24, the "time" is when *we* choose to pray — believe that you receive them *when YOU pray.*

What We Are To Believe When We Pray

...when ye pray, believe that ye receive them...

What did Jesus tell us to believe? Are we to believe in God? Are we to believe that God can do anything? Are we to believe in healing and miracles? Are we to believe in prayer?

Certainly we believe in God. We do believe that God can

do anything. We believe in healing and miracles. And we believe in prayer. *But this is not specifically what Jesus is telling us to believe here.* These beliefs are already understood in this verse. In other words, the reason we're praying is because we do believe in prayer, we do believe in God, and we believe that God can do anything.

The question, though, is, what did Jesus tell us to believe *here in this verse*? The answer is that Jesus told us to *"believe that we receive **them.** "* What is this "them" that Jesus wants us to believe that we receive? The answer is that "thing" we have been desiring — *"What **things** so ever ye desire. "*

Next question — When we pray, what are we to believe about that desire? The answer, according to Jesus, is we are to believe that we *receive* that desire.

What Does The Word "Receive" Mean?

The definition for the word "receive" simply means, *"to get. "* For example, in a game of football the quarterback will send player #80 into the end zone to *receive* the football. After the hike, #80 runs into the end zone and the quarterback throws the ball to him. While the ball is in the air the whole stadium full of people will hold their breath to see if #80 will receive it. (#80 is paid thousands of dollars to receive footballs, which is why he is called a *"receiver.")* If he catches the ball it means he *"receives"* the football. In other words, *he "gets" the ball, it's in his possession, he's got it.*

If I mail a letter to a friend, a week later I might ask my friend, *"Did you receive my letter? "* In other words, I'm asking, *"Did you get my letter?"* Or, *"Do you have the letter I sent you in your possession?"*

When we *receive* a fax from a business we *get* a fax from a business. When we *receive* a phone call we *get* a phone call. When we *receive* a vote of confidence it means we *get* a vote of confidence. When we *receive* a free gift it means we *get* a free gift.

As you can see, the word "receive" means, *"to obtain, to get, to get in one's possession."* So when Jesus says, *"when you pray, believe that you receive them,"* he is saying, *"when you pray, believe that your desire is now in your possession."* Taking our definition from chapter 1 for the word "believe," it would read like this — *"when you pray, accept it as being true without any physical proof that your desire is now in your possession."*

3) ...and ye shall have them.

Before we can "have" them, we first must believe that our desire is in our possession. In other words, we have to believe that we've got it before we get it. Notice the order:

...when ye pray, believe...

When does the "believing" take place? The answer is at the exact same time as the praying. Then:

...believe that ye receive them, and ye shall have them.

When will we "have" it? The answer is *after* we believe

that it is in our possession. In other words, we will have it *after* we first believe we've got it.

The word "shall" ("...and ye *shall* have them") has two meanings. 1) It denotes simple future time, and 2) it denotes certainty, necessity, a definite happening. For example, once we believe that we have it, the next event is that it is a *certainty* we will have it. It will *definitely* come to pass. According to Jesus, the eventual outcome is a *surety*, it is *inevitable*. We have Jesus' word that we, most definitely, *shall* have it.

Then, too, the word "shall" is a future tense word. In other words, the *"having"* is future from *"when we pray."* It is the "believing that we receive it" that takes place when we pray, *not the having.* The "having" comes sometime *after* we pray, *whether it's 3 seconds, 3 minutes, 3 hours or 3 days.* According to Jesus, once we believe that we have it, the next event is that it will come to pass.

Thus, to insert these definitions into Mark 11:24, it would read like this — **"What things soever you desire, when you pray, accept it as being true without any physical proof that you get your desire into your possession, and it will most definitely come to pass."**

The purpose of the prayer is to "have" it, that is, to see and feel it. Thus, Jesus is telling us that we first have to believe that we have it without any feeling or seeing *in order to produce the feeling and seeing.* This is why God recorded the cursing of the fig tree — to give us an example of what He was talking about. Remember, when Jesus cursed the fig tree *there wasn't any evidence to the sight* that anything had taken place. Jesus *believed* that the tree was dead even though there wasn't any physical proof that could be seen with the eye.

What The Word "Believe" Means

This is why 2 Corinthians 5:7 tells us to walk by faith and not by sight. Sight would say that it's not true, whereas faith would say that it is true. The key word is "believe." Jesus said, *"when you pray, **believe** that you receive them."* Notice what Jesus said on another occasion:

> **Jesus saith unto him, Thomas, because thou hast seen me, thou hast believed:** *blessed are they that have not seen, and yet have believed.*
> **- John 20:29**

The kind of believing that has the blessing of God attached to it is to believe *without seeing.* When we believe without seeing, it will produce the seeing. Yet until it is seen, it is no less true while it's unseen. *Jesus would not tell us to believe that we have it if it were not true.*

For example, just because the disciples couldn't see that the fig tree was dead it didn't mean that the tree wasn't dead. Just because Thomas didn't see that Jesus was alive the first week after the resurrection it didn't mean that Jesus wasn't alive. Just because the Syrians in 2 Kings 6:16-17 didn't see the angels surrounding Elisha it didn't mean that the angels weren't there.

If Jesus told us to believe that God answered our prayer, it

38

must be true even though we can't see or feel it. But by believing that we have it, Jesus said that we will have it in this realm of seeing and feeling.

CHAPTER
4

BELIEVING THE UNSEEN

Now faith is...the evidence of things *not seen*.
- Hebrews 11:1

There's a difference between saying that a thing doesn't exist and saying that a thing is not seen. Just because something can't be seen it doesn't mean that it doesn't exist. For example, we can't see the wind, yet there's no doubt that it exists. We can't see the air we breathe, yet it exists. We can't see an atom, yet it exists. We can't see bacteria, yet it exists. Likewise, faith has to do with things that can't be seen, yet exist. As we saw with the fig tree, the tree was just as dead when it couldn't be seen as it was when it could be seen.

Another good example of this is found in the gospel of John chapter 4. The father of a dying son had to believe that his son was well even though he couldn't see that his son had been healed. When the father first came to Jesus to ask him to heal his son, he fell into the trap that everyone falls into when they first hear about faith. He wanted to see some sign that his son was healed. Jesus even said to the man:

Except ye see signs and wonders, ye will not believe.
- John 4:48

It's a common mistake to want to believe only what we can see. The problem with this, though, is that it doesn't please God. The father then implored Jesus to again come heal his son. But Jesus simply stated, *"Go thy way; thy son liveth."* The father was now faced with a decision. He could walk away dejected without the physical confirmation that he desired, or he could go home with a song in his heart because he *believed* that what Jesus said was true. The father wisely chose the latter.

...And the man *believed* the word that Jesus had spoken unto him, and he went his way.
- John 4:50

This father took a leap over what he could see and chose to believe what was said by Jesus. Because his home was a considerable distance away it wasn't until the next day that he was close to home. He had the opportunity over the night to refuse to be moved by the impending death of his son. Because Jesus said that he would live, he could believe that his son would live. It didn't matter that he couldn't see if his son was healed, he now had an evidence of words that said his son was healed. It was just as true as if he could see it. Again, faith is the evidence of things not seen. The healing of his son was no less true when he could see it as it was when he couldn't see it.

The next day, as this father was getting close to home, his servants met him and informed him that his son was going to live.

Then inquired he of them the hour when he began to amend. And they said unto him, Yesterday at the seventh hour the fever left him. So the father _KNEW_ that it was at the same hour, in which Jesus said unto him, Thy son liveth...

- John 4:52-53

Knowing will always follow believing, not vice-versa. The father first _believed_ that his son was healed, then the next day he _knew_ that his son was healed. Because he chose to believe what couldn't be seen, his faith produced that which could be seen. Like many others, he first wanted to know before he would believe, but the rebuke from Jesus straightened out his thinking and he chose to believe. His reward for believing was the knowing of his son's healing.

Another important point in this story is the fact that his son _began to amend._

Then inquired he of them the hour WHEN HE BEGAN TO AMEND...

- John 4:52

Had the father been at his son's side when Jesus spoke the

word of healing he still would've had to believe. Though the fever left the son when Jesus spoke, the son was still apparently just as weak after Jesus spoke as he was before Jesus spoke. Instead of *immediately* getting better, the son *progressively* got better. There was a time period of recovery that started after Jesus spoke. This is further confirmation that, like with the fig tree, faith believes that God answers when we pray, in spite of what can be seen.

Faith Versus Sight

For we walk by faith, not by sight.
-2 Corinthians 5:7

To walk by faith means that we're not walking by sight. To walk by sight means that we're not walking by faith. According to the apostle Paul, it's impossible to walk by faith and by sight at the same time. One will always have the preeminence over the other. It's up to us to choose which one we'll walk by. Of course, we should rightly choose to walk by faith, because faith has the power to produce sight. Sight doesn't have the power to produce faith. The father of the dying son learned this lesson in the nick of time.

Also, there are two kinds of information alluded to in this verse — information that is based on faith, and information that is based on sight. Faith-information is information that is based on God's Word, because faith can only come by hearing God's Word (Romans 10:17). Sight-information is information that is based on the 5 physical senses — what we see, feel, smell, taste, and hear. Faith-information is the highest source of information, because God's Word is the highest source of information. Sight-information is extremely limited information.

Certainly sight information is necessary, provided it doesn't contradict the highest source of information, God's Word. If it contradicts God's Word, then it's up to us to shift from sight to faith. In other words, for the Christian, information that is based on God's Word is more important than information that is based on sight.

So if sight information tells us we're sick, we must shift from that information to the higher information, God's Word. Since God's Word states, *"by whose stripes ye were healed,"* the only way to obtain the results of this truth would be to shift our walking from the sight-information to the faith-information. We walk by faith, not by sight. The following analogy will help:

Microscope Analogy

We take the microscope for granted today, but for thousands of years the only information man had available to him was what he could gain with the naked eye. Then someone hit upon the idea of a microscope. All of sudden we became aware of a whole different world — microscopic and ultramicroscopic animal and vegetable organisms. We learned of bacteria and viruses.

We found that a person's arm could *look* healthy and strong to the naked eye, but when the skin was put under a microscope it turned out to be diseased and infected. That's when the world learned that the information based on what could be seen with the naked eye was _limited_ information. That kind of information _appeared_ to be correct, but we now had an instrument capable of giving us a higher, more accurate source of information. *So we then walked by microscopic information, not by naked-eye information.* Naked-eye information was limited information.

Do you see how this analogy works? It's alright to live by naked-eye information, that is, unless it contradicts microscopic information. If it contradicts microscopic information, then it's necessary to shift from the naked-eye information to the higher, more accurate microscopic information. One might look and feel well, but the microscope could reveal something that the naked eye couldn't detect.

This is exactly how it is with God's Word. Just as the microscope is a higher, more accurate source of information than the naked eye, *God's Word is a higher, more accurate source of information than the microscope.* Actually, God's Word is the _highest_ source of information. Regardless of what our body may say, there is a more accurate diagnosis than what our body is telling us. For example, if sight-information tells us our body is sick and going to die, then we should put our body under the microscope of God's Word, so to speak, and see that it says, *"by whose stripes ye were healed."*

God's Word Is The Ultimate Microscope

The ultimate microscope is the Word of God. It reveals things that the eye can't detect. Even in the natural, sight-information is unreliable. That's why there are such things as the microscope. We have to get to the real truth besides what

46

we can see. Everything takes a backseat, so to speak, to the Word of God. God's Word is the ultimate truth.

Our body may tell us that we're sick, but the microscope of God's Word says that we're healed. Our bank may tell us that we're broke, but the microscope of God's Word tells us that our needs are supplied. The world may tell us that we don't have anything to look forward to but the grave, but the microscope of God's Word tells us that in the ages to come He's going to show us the exceeding riches of His grace.

The fact that we're told to walk by faith and not by sight shows us that there are going to be times when sight will look contrary to what faith says. We're being taught *ahead of time* to stay with what faith says regardless of how sight may look. **We are to walk by the microscope of God's Word, and not by sight.** God's Word will prevail over all that can be seen.

CHAPTER 5

SEEN THINGS ARE TEMPORARY

While we look not at the things which are seen, but at the things which are not seen: FOR THE THINGS WHICH ARE SEEN ARE TEMPORAL; but things which are not seen are eternal.
- 2 Corinthians 4:18

According to Jesus in Mark 11:24, when we pray, we are to *believe* that we receive our desire. In other words, we are to accept it as being true without any physical proof that we receive our desire. Regardless of what we still see or feel after prayer, God wants us to believe that we've obtained it. At this point, we shouldn't look at what we see, only at what we believe.

While we look not at the things which are seen...
- 2 Corinthians 4:18

This is as clear as it gets. Our faith shouldn't be based on things which are seen. Paul emphatically tells us not to look

49

at the things which are seen. Then notice:

...but at the things which are NOT SEEN.

Our faith should be based on things that are not seen, that which we *believe* God has done. Here's one reason why:

...for the things which are seen are TEMPORAL; but the things which are not seen are ETERNAL.

Everything that can be seen is temporary. The basic definition of "temporary" according to the *Webster's Revised Unabridged Dictionary* (1913) is, *"existing for a limited time."* In other words, when we believe that we receive them, what can still be seen after prayer will exist only for a limited time. It is temporary. Again, we shouldn't be downcast if or when things haven't changed after prayer, this is the time to believe and rejoice. All that can be seen will exist only for a limited time.

An excellent example of this is found in Mark chapter 9. A father had a son who was a lunatic. He first brought his son to the disciples and then to Jesus seeking help:

When Jesus saw that the people came running together, he rebuked the foul spirit, saying unto him, Thou dumb and deaf spirit, I charge thee, come out of him, and enter no more into him. And the spirit cried, AND RENT HIM SORE, and came out of him; INSOMUCH THAT MANY SAID, HE IS DEAD.
- Mark 9:25-26

After Jesus ministered to this father's son, instead of this young man immediately getting better, *he immediately got worse!* Jesus had commanded this spirit to come out of him, yet it doesn't say it just rent him, it says it rent him *sore*. In other words, it wasn't a pretty sight. It looked extremely bad. In fact, many of the onlookers in the crowd actually thought that the boy was dead. I would suppose that's about as bad as a situation could look. Think about this — after being ministered to by Jesus this young man *appeared* to be dead.

This is surprising to some Christians. Some have thought that every person Jesus ministered to was immediately healed. But this wasn't always the case. As we saw with the nobleman's son in John chapter 4, he *began to amend* after Jesus had healed him. With the 10 lepers who were healed by Jesus in Luke chapter 17, they began to get better after they had left Jesus and were on their way to the temple. With the fig tree that Jesus had cursed in Mark chapter 11, it wasn't until the following day that the results of the dead tree could be seen.

These are striking illustrations that we need to learn from. We shouldn't ever be shaken if or when things don't look better after prayer. Again, this young man immediately got worse.

This is so important. Jesus was never shaken by anything he saw. Being a man of faith, he believed that the young man was now set free. Notice verse 27:

But Jesus took him by the hand, and lifted him up; and he arose.

This young man's body was lying on the ground strangely silent. Jesus then took hold of the limp, lifeless-looking hand and began lifting the body to an erect position. At this point the young man responded and he was able to stand under his own strength.

As far as Jesus was concerned, everything negative about this young man that could be seen was only going to exist for a limited time. He wasn't looking at what could be seen, he was looking at what couldn't be seen. He was moved only by what he believed.

This is a truth worthy of more study. If we'll simply believe that we receive our desire when we pray, the problem that can be seen will exist only for a limited time. Another definition of "temporary" is, *"something that is subject to change."* In other words, all things to be prayed about that can be seen, or rather, all sickness, poverty, and difficulties, are subject to change.

For example, the sickness or disease that you may see or feel in your body is subject to change. Unpaid bills, fore-closures, financial difficulties, bankruptcies, etc. are subject to change. Simply put, everything that can be seen __can__ be changed.

Also, it's important to realize that all of the promises of God are eternal. This includes healing, prosperity, peace of mind, etc. These promises won't exist for only a limited time, nor are they subject to change. They exist *forever*, and they're __not__ subject to change. All that is revealed in God's Word, or it could be said, all of the unseen things that God's Word tells us about, are more solid than anything that can be seen. Why? Because they're not subject to change. Health and healing is more solid than sickness and disease, and Biblical prosperity is more solid than financial poverty.

Unseen Things Are Real

Now faith is the substance of THINGS hoped for, the evidence of THINGS not seen.

- Hebrews 11:1

While we look not at the THINGS which are seen, but at the THINGS which are not seen: for the THINGS which are seen are temporal; but the THINGS which are not seen are eternal.

- 2 Corinthians 4:18

Things are not just ideas, nor are they just imaginations, and neither are they pipe-dreams. Things are definite, real, true objects! For example, on the negative side, a tumor is a thing. A germ or virus is a thing. A blind eye is a thing. An ulcer is a thing. An unpaid bill is a thing. But, thank God, those things are temporal and subject to change.

On the positive side, the healing power of God is a thing. The nine gifts of the Spirit listed in 1 Corinthians chapter 12 are things. A supernatural idea from heaven to produce money on earth is a thing. The many, many promises throughout God's Word are things. The good news is, THESE UNSEEN THINGS IN GOD'S WORD ARE GREATER THAN THE SEEN THINGS IN THIS WORLD. And it's our responsibility to look at these unseen things:

While we look...at the things which are not seen...
- 2 Corinthians 4:18

How do we look at things which are not seen? The answer is simple — We look at unseen things through the viewfinder of God's Word. Though the *natural* eye can't see these unseen things, with the ultimate instrument of God's Word, the *eye-of-faith* can. God's Word is God's way of looking at unseen things.

To use healing as a further example, when we pray, we shouldn't be sad if we don't feel better or if we don't look different. God's Word unequivocally states that we are healed. Our responsibility is to now look at the healing that belongs to us in the unseen, eternal realm until it manifests in this seen, temporary realm. By our continuing to look with the eye-of-faith at what God's Word says is ours is what will cause it to manifest in this seen realm.

We need to remind us that just because we can't see or feel something it doesn't mean that it doesn't exist. Again, faith doesn't have anything to do with things that *don't exist*, faith has to do with things *not seen*. True faith is based on the reality of God's Word. It is based on facts.

Faith Is Different Than Sight

For example, sight says that heaven doesn't exist. Since we can't see heaven with a telescope or with a satellite, it must not be. Faith, though, says that heaven does exist. We may not see it, but it's out there somewhere. Why? Because the Bible says it exists. If we would walk by sight, we would

54

say that heaven doesn't exist. If we walk by faith in God's Word, we would say that heaven does exist. Obviously, faith and sight are not the same thing. We can't walk by faith and by sight at the same time.

The same is true with divine healing. If you've prayed for healing, sight may say that you don't have your healing. Since you can't see your healing nor feel your healing, you must not be healed. Faith, though, says that you are healed. You may not see or feel it, but it belongs to you. Why? Because 1 Peter 2:24 says that it's yours. So if we walk by sight we would say that we're not healed. If we walk by faith, we would say that we are healed. Again, faith and sight are not the same thing.

What Faith Is And Is Not

Let me tell you what faith is not. Faith is not an emotion. Faith is not a strong will power. Faith is not something we physically or mentally work us up to. Faith is not magical. Faith is not mystical. And faith is not ooey-gooey, nor like abracadabra.

Let me tell you what faith has to do with. Faith has to do with evidence. Faith has to do with substance. Faith has to do with things that truly exist that are not yet seen with the physical eye.

For example, we can't see the streets of gold in heaven, but our faith states that they must be there, *because God's Word says that they're there*. If we've prayed for healing, yet we can't see or feel our healing yet, our faith states we are healed, *because 1 Peter 2:24 says that we are*. If we've prayed for finances to meet a need, yet we don't have the money in our hands, our faith states that our needs are met, *because Philippians 4:19 says it is so.*

Faith in the promise of God is the evidence that we rely upon after we've prayed until we actually have our answer. Faith takes the place of our healing until we feel well. Faith takes the place of our provision until the money is in our hands. Faith takes our place until we're actually walking on those streets of gold.

Faith always has to do with the unseen. When we can actually see the streets of gold we won't need our faith for them. When we actually feel better we won't need faith for healing. When all the bills are paid we won't need faith for provision. In short, when we can see it, we don't need faith for it. When we can't see it, we need to use our faith until we do see it. Faith is what takes the place of something we can't see until it can be seen.

Back to our healing example — If we're sick in our body, we say, *"1 Peter 2:24 states, 'by whose stripes I'm healed,' therefore I believe I'm healed."* Then, from the time we pray until the time we actually feel good is when our faith comes into play. Our faith is the evidence of our healing while we still feel bad. Until we actually feel better, our faith is our evidence that says we're truly healed during that time. To quote the writer of Hebrews, *"faith is the evidence of things not seen."* What can be seen will now exist for only a limited time.

SECTION 2

SAYING

CHAPTER 6

FAITH IS RELEASED BY SPEAKING

And Jesus said unto them...If ye have faith...ye shall say...

- Matthew 17:20

To preach only the believing of faith without the speaking of faith is to preach only half of what faith is. Faith is released by believing *and saying*. We *say* what we believe. It won't work by believing one thing and saying another thing. Our mouth must work in conjunction with our heart. We must say the same thing that we believe.

Really, faith is not a complex thing. It's very simple. Many have tended to make it complicated, but it was never intended by God to be difficult. The problem has been in trying to work the force of faith by a set of rules other than the ones God has set.

For example, using sports as an analogy, if someone held a football in one hand and an instruction booklet on basketball in the other, they would definitely have a problem. If they try to bounce a football repeatedly like a basketball they're going to think that the game of basketball is an extremely difficult game. Why? Because a football wasn't made to be bounced and dribbled like a basketball. It can't be controlled in that way. An NFL football can't be played with NBA rules. Yes, they may have an official football, but they're trying it with a wrong set of rules.

Likewise, the person who is trying to use their faith by a set of rules other than the ones God has set is going to think that the power of faith is an extremely difficult thing to master. It's like using a football to play basketball. And this is where many sincere people have missed it. They need to be given the correct set of rules.

Plainly, Jesus said, *"If you have faith, you shall say...".* According to Jesus then, if we intend to use our faith we're going to have to *say* something. If we refuse to say something, or if we don't know that we're to say something, our belief will wither away. Beliefs need action, and the primary way our beliefs are released are through what we say.

Our example here in Matthew 17:20, Jesus said, *"If ye have faith...ye shall say."* On another occasion in Luke 17:6, using a sycamine tree as an example, Jesus said the same thing, *"If ye had faith...ye might say...".* In Mark 11:22-23, Jesus said, *"Have faith in God. For verily I say unto you, That whosoever shall say...".* In Matthew 21:21, Jesus said, *"If ye have faith and doubt not...ye shall say...".*

Faith Is Released By Speaking

In each of these four scriptures Jesus associated the using of faith with the saying of something. Not one time did he say that just the having of faith would remove mountains or sycamine trees. In every instance Jesus said that the having of faith was to be acted upon by saying something.

One reason this needs to be taught is because people have mistakenly said, *"I know I've got faith, yet I can't ever get my healing."* But just having faith isn't enough. That's like saying, *"I've got all the food I'll ever need, but why am I so hungry?"* Well, just having food isn't enough. We have to do something with that food in order not to be hungry. We have to eat it. Likewise, we have to do something with our faith in order to receive a miracle. We have to use it. According to Jesus in these verses, we use our faith by saying something.

Others have said, *"If I think positive thoughts everything will work out,"* or *"If I believe good things in bad situations everything will work out."* But not one time did Jesus ever say, "If you believe, the mountain will go away." He did say, though, *"If you believe that those things which you say shall come to pass, you shall have whatsoever you say"* (Mark 11:23).

What Paul Said About Saying

We having the same spirit of faith, according as it is written, I believed, _and therefore have I spoken_; we also believe, _and therefore speak_.
- the apostle Paul, 2 Corinthians 4:13

The apostle Paul is saying the same thing that Jesus said.

If we believe, we must speak. Not only did Paul say that speaking what we believe is according to what is written in scripture, he added his testimony by stating, *"we also believe, and therefore speak."* The scripture he was quoting is found in the book of Psalms:

> **I believed, therefore have I spoken.**
> **- Psalm 116:10**

Paul called this the spirit of faith. Faith believes, and because it believes, it speaks what it believes. If we choose only to believe without speaking, we're not using our faith according to the Word of God. As a result, very little, if anything, will be accomplished.

On another occasion, in his letter to the church in Rome, not only did Paul call believing and speaking the word of faith, he said it's the word of faith that *he and the apostles* preached:

> **But what saith it? The word is nigh thee, even in thy _mouth_, and in thy _heart_: that is, _the word of faith which WE preach_.**
> **- Romans 10:8**

We in the church need to be concerned with the fundamentals of faith the way **_they_** preached them. Clearly, _they_ preached that faith works when it's in two places — in the heart and in the mouth. It not only moves mountains, sycamine trees, and fig trees, as Jesus stated, it also works on the greatest miracle that man has need of — salvation. Notice the very next verse:

That if thou shalt <u>*confess with thy MOUTH*</u> the Lord Jesus, and shalt <u>*BELIEVE in thine heart*</u> that God hath raised him from the dead, thou shalt be saved.
- Romans 10:9

Faith for receiving salvation works just like faith for receiving answers to prayer — by saying with our mouth what we believe in our heart. We first believe that Jesus was raised from the dead, and then we say with our mouth that Jesus is our Lord. Lest there be any doubt about the importance of what we say, Paul settled this issue once and for all in the next verse:

For with the heart man believeth unto righteousness; AND WITH THE MOUTH CONFESSION IS MADE UNTO SALVATION.
- Romans 10:10

Salvation cannot take place until we say with our mouth what we believe in our heart. To say that salvation can take place by only believing without saying is to be completely disrespectful to the scriptures. Incidentally, the word confession in this verse is not talking about the confession of sin. Confession of sin is talked about in 1 John 1:9 where we ask God to forgive us of our sins by our recognizing with our mouth when we sinned. Here in Romans 10:9-10, we are to confess, that is, we are to recognize with our mouth that Jesus is Lord.

The Greek word translated confession here is ***homologeo***. It simply means, *"to speak the same thing."* It's a very strong word that *personalizes* what is said. For example, we don't

63

just say that Jesus is Lord, we say from the *heart* that Jesus is our Lord. This same Greek word is found in Hebrews 10:23 where it says, *"Let us hold fast the <u>profession</u> of our faith...".* This word "profession" would be better translated "confession." We should hold fast to the <u>saying</u> of what we believe. Regardless of the pressure that would come to make us stop saying what we believe, we are to tenaciously keep saying what we believe.

This law of faith, as revealed by Jesus and Paul, works on mountains, sycamine trees, fig trees, salvation, healing, the promises of God, etc. Everything that is received from God is received by faith. Hebrews chapter 11 lists the many accomplishments that faith wrought in past years, a wide diversity of examples from having babies (v.11) to subduing kingdoms (v.33) to stopping the mouths of lions (v.33) to building an ark (v.7) to obtaining promises (v.33). Over and over the phrase "by faith" is used — *"By faith Enoch...", "By faith Noah...", "By faith Abraham...", "Through faith Sarah...", "By faith Isaac...", "By faith Jacob...", "By faith Joseph...", "By faith Moses...", "By faith Rahab...".*

Hebrews 11:33 has always meant much to me — *"Who through faith...obtained promises...".* When I was younger I never knew if I'd be in a position where I would want to remove a mountain or a sycamine tree or part a river (or would even have to). I did know that learning to receive the promises of God would have to be a priority. Actually, Jesus is talking about us removing the mountains of difficulties, so to speak, in our lives — the mountain of debt, the mountain of cancer, the mountain of diabetes, etc. But there's no doubt that if we were in a situation where a literal mountain would have to move, it could be done.

The law of faith is that we believe and speak — *"For with the heart man believeth...and with the mouth confession is made unto..."*. Using salvation as an example, it would read, *"For with the heart man believeth unto righteousness, and with the mouth confession is made unto salvation."* Using healing as an example, it would read, *"For with the heart man believeth unto healing, and with the mouth confession is made unto health."* Using Biblical prosperity as an example, it would read, *"For with the heart man believeth unto increase, and with the mouth confession is made unto prosperity."*

Salvation, healing, and prosperity, etc. will only come to pass when we believe and speak. We believe we're saved, healed, and prosperous, and we *say* we're saved, healed, and prosperous.

What Do We Say?

Faith always says what God says. If we believe that we have received our healing, we must then *say*, *"I believe I have received my healing."* If we believe that God has undertaken our finances, we must *say*, *"I believe that my needs are met according to His riches in glory by Christ Jesus."* If we believe that God has answered our prayer, we must *say*, *"I believe that God has answered my prayer."*

IF WE BELIEVE IT, WE HAVE TO SPEAK IT.

...and CALLETH those things which be not as though

they were.

- Romans 4:17

This verse doesn't say, "...and *thinketh* those things which be not as though they were," and it doesn't say, "...and *believeth* those things which be not as though they were." Of course, we need our minds to think this way, and we certainly need to believe this way, but the point is, Romans 4:17 says to **CALL** those things which be not as though they were. In other words, we've got to **_say_** it. It's not enough to think it, and it's not enough to believe it. We've got to **_say_** with our mouth what we believe in our heart. Faith is released by speaking.

If we need healing, we must **_say_**, *"by Jesus' stripes I am healed."* If we need our bills paid, we must **_say_**, *"according to God's Word my needs are met."* If we need an answer to prayer, we believe and **_say_**. We are taking authority over our circumstances by releasing our faith through what we say.

CHAPTER 7

WORDS ARE POWERFUL

For she SAID, If I may touch but his clothes, I shall be whole.
- woman with the issue of blood,
Mark 5:28

Daughter, THY FAITH hath made thee whole.
- Jesus, Mark 5:34

What we say can make a difference in whether we live or die. Our words reveal what's in our heart. This woman's words brought to light the faith that was in her heart. She believed that if she could get to Jesus and touch his clothes she would be healed. She then acted on her belief by saying it and doing it. It should be noted that the initial response to her belief was to say something. *What she said was her faith speaking.*

Had this woman said, *"I don't know if I'll ever be healed. I have no guarantee that I'll even be able to get to Jesus. I've*

67

suffered for so long. I might as well stay here and at least die in peace." Had she talked that way she would have died. Her words would have caused her to focus on death instead of on life. She would have talked herself out of any possibility of getting well.

Words are very powerful. They either imprison us or set us free. They bring healing or sickness, prosperity or poverty, and success or defeat. Our words lead the direction that our lives will follow. The apostle James even compared the tongue to a rudder on a ship.

> **Behold also the ships, which though they be so great, and are driven of fierce winds, YET ARE THEY TURNED ABOUT WITH A VERY SMALL HELM ...EVEN SO THE TONGUE IS A LITTLE MEMBER...**
> **- James 3:4-5**

It's remarkable how something as small as a rudder can affect something as colossal as a ship, even in the midst of fierce winds. The direction that the rudder is pointed is the direction that the ship will go. If the helmsman turns the rudder to the left, the ship will move toward the left. If the helmsman turns the rudder to the right, the ship will turn toward the right.

Likewise, the tongue, as small as it is, affects not just our bodies, but our whole lives as well. The words that we speak establish the direction that our lives will start traveling. If we talk defeat, our lives will move toward unfulfilled and unproductive lives. If we talk poverty, our finances will move toward decrease and lack. If we talk sickness and disease, our bodies will move away from health and healing toward sickness and disease.

This is why it's critical to put a guard on our mouths, if necessary, to keep from saying things that we ought not to be saying. Just because a doubt or fear comes to our mind it doesn't mean that we should speak it. We should never speak things that we don't want to come to pass.

For example, if a person is afraid of getting cancer, they should never say, *"I'm afraid I've got cancer."* The person who says such things is unwittingly moving his or her life in the very direction that they want to avoid. The person who is always talking about his fears is keeping his life bound in the very thing he can't stand. The parent who continually says, *"My kids will never amount to anything,"* is unknowingly molding their child for a dismal and bleak future. The writer of Proverbs puts it this way:

Death and life are in the power of the tongue...
- Proverbs 18:21

Another way to say this is:

Death and life are in the power of *what we say*...

Or:

Death and life are in the power of our *words*...

What we continually say will ultimately result in death or life. If we ignorantly talk about fear, sickness, disease, poverty, and doubt, our lives will move away from life toward death. The words *"I can't"* should be removed from our vocabularies. It's sad to hear a person continually saying, *"I can't do this,"* or *"I can't do that."* Though they think they are talking about their present skills or past abilities, they're really stifling their future possibilities. The person who consistently says, *"I can't"* will never put forth any effort to even try.

According to the writer of Proverbs, there is power in the words that we speak. This power is either going to work *for* us, or it's going to work *against* us. To give us an idea of the extremity of this power, this verse says that our words will actually result in death or life. Our words will generate life for us, or they'll bring death to us. It's simply up to us, knowingly *or unknowingly.* Whatever it is that we're saying will be the eventual end result.

It's amazing how some people choose to disregard scriptures such as these. They say, *"I don't think it's all that important what I say. I've lived as long as I've lived by talking the way that I've been talking, and I'm still alive."* That's like the person who says, *"I've been smoking cigarettes all my life, and I'm still alive. So I don't think it matters whether or not I smoke cigarettes."* But just because they don't have lung cancer or heart disease yet it doesn't mean that each cigarette they smoke isn't taking its toll — little by little and minute by minute off their life. We cannot ignore statistics.

It's like the proverbial straw that broke the camel's back. Obviously, one straw won't break a camel's back. The lesson is, by adding pound after pound after pound, there will come a point when, as strong as a camel's back is, it will hit its breaking point. When it does, it doesn't matter if the final weight is just a gnat, feather, or straw, that camel is going to buckle and collapse. It's not the final straw that's the problem. It's the accumulation of all the added weight over time that's the problem. Sooner or later, it will take its toll. So just because everything has *seemed* to be alright with them for a number of years *it doesn't mean that everything is alright.*

Our words do two things. 1) Our words are the outgrowth of what's on the inside of us. In other words, they reveal what's *already* on the inside of us. For example, people who are worried are always talking about what they're worried about. People who are depressed are always talking about what's got them depressed. People who are fearful are always talking about what they're afraid of. And, 2) Our words are the rudder that controls the direction our lives will take. So the people who are unhappy with the direction their lives have been heading need to move their rudder, so to speak, by changing what they're saying.

Our words are either adding to our lives little by little, or our words are taking away from our lives little by little. Our words are either opening the door to blessing and closing the door to cursing, or our words are closing the door to blessing and opening the door to cursing. Just because we can't immediately see any outward change that's either good or bad it doesn't mean that there aren't profound changes taking place in our lives behind-the-scenes either good or bad. What we say is just as important as what we believe. One is not more important than the other, both are just as important as the other. This is why it's so important to speak only words inspired by faith.

David Spoke Faith Words

When the giant Goliath confronted the children of Israel, David refused to be intimidated. He believed that because Goliath defied Israel he was defying God. David decided to go against Goliath in the name of the Lord and boldly spoke what he believed.

1 Samuel 17
26 AND DAVID SPAKE to the men that stood by him, SAYING, What shall be done to the man that killeth this Philistine, and taketh away the reproach from Israel? *For who is this uncircumcised Philistine that he should defy the armies of the living God?*

32 AND DAVID SAID to Saul, Let no man's heart fail because of him; thy servant will go and fight this Philistine.

34 AND DAVID SAID unto Saul, Thy servant kept his father's sheep, and there came a lion, and a bear, and took a lamb out of the flock: And I went out after him, and smote him, and delivered it out of his mouth: and when he arose against me, I caught him by his beard, and smote him, and slew him. Thy servant slew both the lion and the bear: *and this uncircumcised Philistine shall be as one of them,* **seeing he hath defied the armies of the living God.**

37 AND DAVID SAID moreover, The Lord that delivered me out of the paw of the lion, and out of the paw of the bear, *he will deliver me out of the hand of this Phili-*

stine.

45 THEN SAID DAVID to the Philistine, Thou comest to me with a sword, and with a spear, and with a shield: *but I come to thee in the name of the Lord of hosts, the God of the armies of Israel, whom thou hast defied.*

46 *This day will the Lord deliver thee into mine hand***; and I will smite thee, and take thine head from thee; and I will give the carcases of the host of the Philistines this day unto the fowls of the air, and to the wild beasts of the earth; that all the earth may know that there is a God in Israel.**

47 And all this assembly shall know that the Lord saveth not with sword and spear: *For the battle is the Lord's, and he will give you into our hands.*

David said what he said for two reasons — 1) Like a rudder on a ship, he was directing this battle in the direction that he wanted it to go, and 2) he believed that he was on God's side with God's help. He believed that before the day would end, Goliath would be flat on his back dead. His words were simply releasing the faith that was in his heart. Because death and life are in the power of the tongue, David was taking full advantage of all that God was providing.

Speaking our faith is vital to success. People of success have learned to stay away from speaking fears and doubts. Negative speaking is only counterproductive to what we want to accomplish. It affects the people we work with, our own attitude, and allows fear and doubt to gain the ascendency in any given situation. Just from the natural standpoint, every person has certain strengths and weaknesses, and it doesn't make sense to live our lives focusing on our weaknesses. If everyone did that nothing would have ever been invented and we'd still be riding in the horse-and-buggy and fighting polio. We need to capitalize on what we can do and on what God has said we can do. We need to live our lives accentuating our strengths and abilities within the framework of God's ability.

This is all the more important in impossible situations. When David faced Goliath his first realization regarding strengths and weaknesses was to refuse Saul's armor and to stick with an expertise that he was comfortable in using, his tried and true shepherd's staff and slingshot. He knew that they had worked before and wouldn't fail him when he needed them most.

Secondly, David didn't fight Goliath in his own name. He was going against Goliath in the name of the Lord of hosts. Over and over he said, *"The Lord will deliver you into my hand," "the battle is the Lord's, and he will give you into our hands," "the Lord will deliver me out of the hand of this Philistine," "I come to thee in the name of the Lord of hosts."* His own ability was subservient to God's ability. In other words, he recognized his own ability with a staff and slingshot, yet he knew it would take God's ability superceding his own to win over Goliath.

His faith was in God's power. David believed that God would be faithful to honor His Word. The same God who brought Israel out of Egypt and delivered him from the paw of the lion and bear would help him to do what needed to be done with Goliath. One truth this scripture repeatedly brings out is that David didn't just *believe* that God was his help, he *said* what he believed. *What he said was his faith speaking*.

The writer of Hebrews puts it this way:

...for he hath said, I will never leave thee, nor forsake thee SO THAT WE MAY BOLDLY _SAY_, The Lord is my _helper_, and I will not fear what man shall do unto me.

- Hebrews 13:5-6

It's not enough to believe that God is our helper, we must boldly _say_ that God is our helper.

Joshua And Caleb Spoke Faith Words

We see this same principal with Joshua and Caleb, two of the twelve spies who were sent by Moses to survey the promised land. They were the only two out of the twelve who spoke words of faith. Because God had told the children of Israel to possess the promised land, Joshua and Caleb believed that they could do what God had said they could do. In addition to believing what God had said, they _spoke_ what they believed.

And Caleb stilled the people before Moses, and SAID, Let us go up at once, and possess it; for we are well able to overcome it.

- Numbers 13:30

This is so important. We must always side in with what God has said by speaking right words. When the difficult circumstances we're in look impossible, it is all the more reason to hold fast to our confession of faith. Anyone can speak positive words when things look easy. But when things appear

75

difficult is when words of faith come in to play. Words of faith have to do with what can't be seen. Words of faith have to do with what God has said, not with what can be seen. Sadly, most people don't or won't do this. Most people are like the other 10 spies who bypassed what God had said and spoke only about how impossible things appeared:

But the men that went up with him SAID, We be not able to go up against the people; for they are stronger than we. ...The land through which we have gone to search it, is a land that eateth up the inhabitants thereof: and all the people that we saw in it are men of great stature. And there we saw the giants, the sons of Anak, which come of the giants: and we were in our own sight as grasshoppers, and so we were in their sight.
- Numbers 13:31-33

Unfortunately, most people are programmed to agree with a negative report. The whole camp of the children of Israel opted to ignore what God had said in favor of what the ten spies had said. Obviously, the majority isn't always right. They later bitterly regretted that decision, because out of the whole camp, only Joshua and Caleb were allowed to enter into the promised land. The scripture called this negative verbal report by the ten spies an *evil* report.

And they brought up an EVIL REPORT of the land which they had searched unto the children of Israel, SAYING...
- Numbers 13:32

This is significant — What they said wasn't simply called

a *bad* report, nor was it called an *ignorant* report, and neither was it called a report of *doubt* and *unbelief*, though it was certainly all of these. **God called what they had said an *evil* report**. This is an incredibly strong choice of a word. God considered this to be *evil*! When we think of all that the Bible labels evil few people would have recognized the seriousness of how important wrong words are. God considers it *evil* to speak words contrary to the revealed Word of God.

Some people say, *"But I can't help it. I always speak what's on my mind."* But they're wrong. We can keep from saying what's on our minds, just as we can keep from doing anything else that the Bible says is evil. Joshua and Caleb did. They saw the same giants, the same fortresses, and the same walled cities, but they chose to say what God said. Their minds comprehended the same impossible odds against victory as the other ten, but they calculated in the ability of God. They chose not to forget how they came out of Egypt and how God had brought them across the Red Sea. They remembered the 10 plagues and the destruction of the Egyptian army. As far as they were concerned, this was another opportunity for God to work on their behalf. They boldly said, *"We are well able to overcome it."* Again, what they said was their faith speaking.

It's interesting to note that 40 years later Joshua was still unintimidated by those giants, the sons of Anak also called the Anakims, that bothered the other ten spies. Joshua finished the job he and Caleb were ready to start 40 years earlier when they came back from spying out the land.

And at that time came Joshua, and cut off the

Anakims from the mountains, from Hebron, from Debir, from Anab, and from all the mountains of Judah, and from all the mountains of Israel: JOSHUA DESTROYED THEM UTTERLY WITH THEIR CITIES. There was none of the Anakims left in the land of the children of Israel...So Joshua took the whole land, according to all that the Lord said unto Moses...

- Joshua 11:21-23

There's no question that the stature of these people had to be imposing, just as Goliath's stature was imposing to the children of Israel in David's day. But faith is unaffected by how imposing the difficult circumstances appear. Joshua said the same thing that he would have said had the Anakims been only 3 feet tall. As far as Joshua was concerned, he wasn't a grasshopper in his own sight. He viewed himself through God's eyes — he was the giant and they were the grasshoppers! Faith sees every situation as God sees it.

Joshua 1:8 is as clear as it gets:

This book of the law (God's Word) SHALL NOT DEPART OUT OF THY MOUTH...

The Woman With The Issue Of Blood Spoke Faith Words

The woman with the issue of blood is another excellent illustration of the power of right speaking and right believing. The odds of her getting well from the human and medical standpoint were nonexistent. The giant she was facing was every bit as life-threatening as the human giants David, Joshua, and Caleb faced. But when she had heard of Jesus, faith came alive in her heart. She believed that if she could get to Jesus she would touch the hem of his garment and be healed. Like David, Joshua, and Caleb she *spoke* what she believed.

For she SAID, If I may touch but his clothes, I shall be whole.
- Mark 5:28

The Greek word translated "said" should more accurately be translated that she "kept saying." She *kept* saying, *"If I may touch but his clothes, I shall be whole."* She not only kept it in her heart, she kept it in her mouth.

We should always keep God's Word in our mouths, *but all the more so when difficult times are upon us.* Some people will talk right when things are going easy, but when the pressure begins to mount, they let loose of their confession of faith. But this is the time that it's so vital to hold fast to speaking what God says. This woman's faith was revealed by the words that she spoke. How do we know? Because Jesus said in verse 34, *"Thy faith hath made thee whole."* What she was saying was her faith speaking.

We can't believe faith and speak fear. Nor can we believe faith and speak doubt. Nor can we believe faith and speak unbelief. *Wrong speaking negates right believing.* As far as God is concerned, it's evil. It keeps us from entering into the promised land of God's promises. It is so necessary to think right, believe right, and speak right. This means that we should *meditate* on God's Word day and night (Joshua 1:8), we should *believe* God's Word in our hearts, and we

79

should *speak* God's Word with our mouths.

Success and victory are obtainable goals. If we've been living defeated lives we need to re-examine what we've been doing and saying. It's absurd to want a brighter future without being willing to change our present, because our present is the composite of our past. If our past hasn't brought a wonderful present, our future won't be any different than the present, that is, unless we're willing to change what we're doing in the present. Words are powerful containers that carry victory, healing, and prosperity, or defeat, sickness, and poverty. Our words can change our future, because they change our present.

CHAPTER
8

CALLING THOSE THINGS WHICH BE NOT AS THOUGH THEY WERE

In Romans chapter 4 the apostle Paul parallels the teaching of Jesus in Mark chapter 11 — we have to believe and say that we've got it before we get it. In Paul's teaching he uses the miracle that God performed in the life of Abraham as his example. The account of this miracle is recorded in Genesis chapter 17, but in Romans chapter 4, Paul lifts the veil, so to speak, and gives us an insight into the spiritual law that was in operation when God spoke with Abraham.

In Genesis chapter 17 we see the *demonstration*, but in Romans 4:17 we get the *explanation*. In other words, this spiritual law is recorded in Genesis 17, but it's revealed in Romans 4:17. God worked the miracle in Genesis 17, but Paul brings to light the inner working of the miracle in Romans 4.

As it is written, (I HAVE MADE THEE a father of many nations,) before him whom he believed, even God, who quickeneth the dead, AND CALLETH THOSE THINGS WHICH BE NOT AS THOUGH THEY WERE...(SO) THAT HE MIGHT BECOME the father of many nations...

- Romans 4:17, 18

Let's briefly recall the situation of Abraham. The desire of Abraham's heart was that he would have a child. He had wanted a child for so long, yet it was physically impossible for him and Sarah to have a child. He was 99 years old, she was 90 years old, and in all their years of married life they had not been able to conceive (according to Genesis 11:30 Sarah was barren). Here in Romans chapter 4 Paul shows us what Abraham did from the time he received the promise to the time he actually had his baby in his arms. Notice the sequence:

...I HAVE MADE THEE a father of many nations...
- God to Abraham, Romans 4:17

It's important to realize that God had made this statement to Abraham *before* Abraham had a child. God didn't say, *"I'm going to make thee a father of many nations,"* but instead said, *"I have made thee a father of many nations."* Notice the order — God first said, *"I **have** (past tense) made you a father of many nations"*, then secondly it said in verse 18 (referring to Abraham), *"Who against hope believed in hope, that he **might become** (future tense) the father of many nations"*.

82

In other words, when God said that he _had_ made Abraham a father of many nations, *from Abraham's viewpoint* he was _not_ a father of many nations. (He didn't even have *one* child yet, let alone a nation full.) But Abraham *chose to believe* that God *had* made him a father of many nations so that he *might become* a father of many nations.

How does this work? For the answer notice again the last part of verse 17:

...and calleth those things which be not as though they were.

According to Paul, this is what God was doing in Genesis 17:5. For clarification, let's take this clause apart:

...and calleth those things which be not...

That is, those things that are _not_ in existence in this physical, natural world. Yet it says that he calleth them...

...as _though_ they were.

In other words, as _though_ they already were in existence in this physical, natural world. Thus, we could read this verse as follows:

...and calleth those things that are not in existence in this physical, natural world as though they already were in existence in this physical, natural world.
- Romans 4:17 (my paraphrase)

For example, in Abraham's case here, the "thing" that did not exist in this natural world was his baby. There wasn't even such a thing as a baby named Isaac. But even though it didn't exist yet, God had called it as though it already did exist. This is why God didn't say, *"I'm going to make you a father of many nations,"* but why He said, *"I have made you a father of many nations."* He was calling something that didn't exist in this world yet as though it already did exist in this world.

This is a spiritual principle *set by God.* God calls things into being by declaring it done. This is what sets the wheels in motion to bring it to pass. Further, this principle didn't work only for Abraham to receive his child, *it's also for you and me* today to receive the promises of God.

For example, if you're in bed sick, it's time to say, *"by Jesus' stripes I am healed."* It's time to call those things which be not as though they were. In other words, your body really is sick, but you're going to call it *as though* it were well. This is how Abraham received his child, and it's how we are going to receive the promises of God.

This Is Not Christian Science

This needs to be clarified. This is *not* New Age. This is *not* Gnosticism. And this is *not* Christian Science. **This is Romans 4:17.** What has happened is that these cults have taken a Biblical truth and perverted it to be some kind of a mind-over-matter trick to meet the selfish desires of the ungodly, and to dupe people into joining their cult. But just because these cults have abused a Biblical principle it doesn't mean that we should stop doing what the Bible says is right! *Errors are not corrected by stopping the truth.* We continue to do what's right regardless of what other people do or don't do. Those who want to know the truth can be helped, but those who don't want to be helped will continue to do what they want to do, regardless of you and me.

The truth is, we're not talking here about mind-over-matter, we're talking about a spiritual principle *set by God* as outlined in Romans 4:17. God desires for all of the needs of his people to be met, so He has given us *"exceeding great and precious promises"* (2 Peter 1:4), and we receive these promises *by faith*. The father of our faith, Abraham, *is our example here in Romans chapter 4* to show us what he did to receive his miracle child so that we would learn how to receive whatever it is that we need or desire from God.

Let's continue at verse 18:

Who against hope believed in hope...

In other words, it was a hopeless situation for Abraham. It was against all reason and was impossible for him to be able to have a baby. But even though there wasn't any hope, Abraham decided to believe God anyway.

The Importance Of Hope

This is why hope is so important. Hope is the goal setter, so to speak. Hope is what sets the goal for what it is that we need or desire. When faith is then added to that hope, this is what brings the hope to pass. As Hebrews 11:1 says, *"...faith*

85

*is the substance of things **hoped for**...*". In other words, if we don't have anything that we're hoping for, we don't have a goal to add our faith to. Faith needs a hope.

For example, if there's something that you've been wanting so bad that you can almost taste it, so to speak, *that's what your hope is.* That's your goal. A teenager's hope might be a car. A sick person's hope would be his healing. A poor person's hope would be to have his bills paid. In Abraham's case, his hope was that he would become a father.

Of course, a hope without faith won't produce any results. Just because a teenager hopes for a car it doesn't mean that he will get a car. A hope by itself is void and empty. Hope needs assurance. It needs substance. That's where faith comes into play. Hope gives fuel to a desire. *Just as a carrot in front of a donkey motivates a donkey to keep going forward, our hope motivates us to keep pressing forward with our faith.* Our hope is a goal. Let's read on:

Who against hope believed in hope, that he might become the father of many nations, according to that which was spoken, So _shall_ thy seed be.
- Romans 4:18

Notice the word "shall" — "*So _shall_ thy seed be.*" This is how God works. He's made two statements here — 1) I *have* made thee a father of many nations (past tense), and 2) So *shall* thy seed be (future tense). Once God makes his declaration it will, sooner or later, come to pass. It *shall* be what God has already declared.

86

For example, since God said that Abraham _was_ a father of many nations, that meant that Abraham truly _was_ a father of many nations _whether or not he had a child_. But because God said that he was a father of many nations, this also meant that Abraham would have a son sometime somewhere.

If God speaks something, whether or not it looks that way from the natural, human standpoint, we can rest assured that it _is_ so, and it _shall_ be (i.e. come to pass) sooner or later in this natural world. This is why when God said, _"I have made thee a father of many nations,"_ he could then say, _"So shall thy seed be."_ In other words, because God _had_ made him a father of many nations, Abraham _was_ going to have a family. His "seed" was a _sure_ thing from that moment forward.

Take, for example, receiving healing. When we receive God's Word on healing, _"by whose stripes ye were healed,"_ and we act on that word in faith by declaring, _"by Jesus' stripes I am healed,"_ from that moment forward our healing _shall_ come to pass. Because we _believe_ that we're healed, we _shall_ "feel" our healing. As it reads in Mark 11:24, _"believe that you receive them, and you shall have them."_

When Abraham believed that he was indeed the father of many nations, God said, _"So shall your seed be."_ The end result was that by the following year he had a son and named him Isaac.

How Does This Apply To Us?

The two word clause in verse 17 _"before him"_ would better be served to be translated _"like unto him."_ A good ref-

erence Bible will point this out in the margin. As such it could
be translated as follows:

**Therefore it is of FAITH, that it might be by grace;
to the end the promise might be sure to ALL the seed; not
to that only which is of the law, but to that also which is of
the faith of Abraham (who)....JUST LIKE WHOM HE
BELIEVED, EVEN GOD, who...CALLETH those things
which be not as though they were.**
- Romans 4:16-17

In other words, just as God called those things which be
not as though they were, Abraham also believed and called
those things which be not as though they were. Clearly,
Abraham did just like God did. God didn't require Abraham
to do something that He didn't do, and God doesn't require us
to do something that He doesn't do. We are the faith children
of a faith God. He created the world by using words, and He
wants us to frame our lives by using right words.

We also see that faith believes *and calls*. Verse 17 doesn't
read, *"...and thinketh those things which be not as though
they were,"* although we certainly should want our minds
thinking this way. Faith doesn't believe and *think*, it believes
and *calls*. In other words, we need to SAY it. It's not enough
to *think* it and it's not enough to *believe* it. God wants us to
say with our mouth what we believe in our heart.

Further, God wants us to say what He's already said about
us. For example, in 1 Peter 2:24, God has already said, *"by
whose stripes ye **were** healed."* He didn't say, *"by whose*

stripes I will heal you. " No, thank God, he said that we *already* were healed (past tense)! In Matthew 8:17 the scripture states, *"Himself **took** our infirmities and bare **our** sicknesses.* " Notice that it doesn't say that He *will* take our infirmities sometime. No, He *already* took them and He *already* bore them. It is so.

Thus, to obtain the results of what God has *already* done and spoken, just like Abraham, we need to receive it by agreeing with God, in spite of how we look or feel. If you're in bed sick, it's time to **SAY** in faith, *"Himself took my infirmities and bare my sicknesses. According to God's Word I am healed.* " If you have an incurable disease, it's time to **SAY** in faith, *"by Jesus' stripes I am healed.* " If your bills are past due, it's time to **SAY** in faith, *"My God supplies all of my need according to his riches in glory by Christ Jesus. I believe that my needs are met.* " By believing and agreeing with what God has already spoken we are allowing God to perform what He has said.

90

CHAPTER
9

5 EXAMPLES OF ROMANS 4:17 IN THE MINISTRY OF JESUS

In the preceding chapter we saw how that Abraham received his miracle child by implementing the spiritual law set by God in which God calls those things which be not as though they were. We also saw that Abraham acted *like* God by also calling those things which be not as though they were. In fact, when God changed Abram's name to Abraham, the very name *"Abraham"* meant *"the father of a multitude."* So although Abram was not a father of many nations, God *called* him a father of many nations *in order to make him a father of many nations.* We saw God's part and Abraham's part.

It's important to realize that Abraham had to participate in order for the miracle to come to pass. Abraham had to believe that he was indeed the father of many nations simply because God had spoken it, even though there wasn't any hope in the natural to verify God's claim. And because he accepted it as truth, the ensuing result was a miracle child one year later (Genesis 17:21).

Some people have thought that they'd be lying if they called those things which be not as though they were. They've said, *"How can I say I'm healed when I know I'm not?"* The answer is simple — We're walking by faith and not by sight. We're not walking by what we _know_, we're walking by what we _believe_. How could we be lying when we're just talking about what we believe?

Was God lying when he said that Abraham was the father of a multitude when he didn't even have one child? Was God lying when he said that Jesus was the lamb slain from the foundation of the world when we know that Jesus wasn't slain until approximately 4,000 years after Adam? Was God lying when he told the children of Israel that the promised land belonged to them when actually the Amalekites and the Canaanites were the ones living in it? Was God lying when He told Elijah that He had commanded a widow woman to sustain him when the widow woman didn't know about any such command and was about to starve? Was Elijah lying when he said that there was a sound of an abundance of rain when there wasn't a cloud in the sky? Was Jesus lying when he told the Laodiceans that they were poor and wretched when actually they were rich and increased with goods?

The answer to these questions is no. Obviously, there are two kinds of truth. There is the truth that is based on that which is seen, and there is the truth that is based on faith. The Laodiceans appeared to be rich and increased with goods, but Jesus was talking about a truth that was on a higher level than the truth that they could see.

In order to come to the place of knowing, we have to cross

the bridge of believing. We're calling those things which be not in this seeing and feeling realm as though they were in the seeing and feeling realm. In other words, we're saying we're healed because we *believe* we're healed. Our conversation and manner of life is centered around what God's Word says instead of the ever fluctuating feelings of the body.

Jesus lived in this realm called faith. Everything that he said and did was based on what God led him to say and do. It didn't make sense to say, *"Before Abraham was, I am,"* when the people looking at him could see that he was only in his early thirties. But he had a truth that they didn't comprehend. All that he said and did was based upon the highest information available that, much of the time, bypassed that which could be seen and felt. Let's look at 5 examples of Jesus in action.

Jesus Called Those Things Which Be Not As Though They Were

1. And, behold, there cometh one of the rulers of the synagogue, Jairus by name; and when he saw him, he fell at his feet, And besought him greatly, saying, My little daughter lieth at the point of death: I pray thee, come and lay thy hands on her, that she may be healed; and she shall live. And Jesus went with him; and much people followed him, and thronged him.

- Mark 5:22-24

Jairus came to Jesus pleading for him to accompany him to his home to heal his only daughter. According to Jairus she was at the point of death. Jesus obliged him by going with him to his house. As they were walking someone came to Jairus with the worst possible news:

>**While he yet spake, there came from the ruler of the synagogue's house certain which said, *Thy daughter is dead*: why troublest thou the Master any further?**
>
>   **- Mark 5:35**

That which Jairus was trying to keep from happening happened — his daughter died. Regrettably, he wasn't present with her in her last precious moments. His grief must have been overwhelming. But listen to Jesus:

>**As soon as Jesus heard the word that was spoken, he saith unto the ruler of the synagogue, Be not afraid, only believe.**
>
>**And when he was come in, he SAITH unto them, Why make ye this ado, and weep? *THE DAMSEL IS NOT DEAD*, BUT SLEEPETH.**
>
>   **- Mark 5:36, 39**

What? Jairus' daughter is clearly dead, yet Jesus is saying that she's not dead, only sleeping. Why would he say such a thing? If she were really dead, why would he say that she's sleeping? Was he denying the truth of what had really happened? Was he ignoring the facts as they really stood?

Of course Jesus wasn't. Jesus fully understood the facts. But he was doing something that was a part of *changing* the facts. He was doing what God had done with Abraham. He was calling those things which be not as *though* they were.

In other words, Jairus' daughter was not alive, she was truly dead, but Jesus was calling it as though she was alive. Just as God had called Abram a father of many nations *before* he actually was, Jesus was calling this girl alive *before* she actually was. God and Jesus both took a situation that "was not" and called it as *though* it was. This is the spiritual law set by God that causes it to *become* what it wasn't just moments before.

2.   He said unto them, Give place: FOR THE MAID IS NOT DEAD, but sleepeth. And they laughed him to scorn.
- Matthew 9:24

This is the same account which we just read about in Mark chapter 5, so there's no need to go into much detail. But because Matthew recorded what Mark recorded it evidently had made an impact on both of them. The girl is undoubtedly dead, yet Jesus took this circumstance that "was not" and called it as though it were.

Notice the last clause of verse 24 — *"And they laughed him to scorn."* For whatever reason, some people don't want to understand certain aspects of the things of God. When you start agreeing with God and calling those things which be not as though they were, some people won't believe *with* you. Some will even go so far as these people in verse 24 to make fun of you and to ridicule you.

Just as Jesus put them out of the house, *we need to put them out of our minds and thinking*. We should never let skeptics influence what we believe. We are to keep doing what God did and to keep saying what the Word of God says.

Just as Jesus' words came to pass, God's Word in our mouths will come to pass, that is, if we believe it in our hearts. And when the miracle materializes, there's not any argument that can stand up to it.

3.   And all wept, and bewailed her: but he (Jesus) said, Weep not; SHE IS NOT DEAD, but sleepeth.

- Luke 8:52

Again, we see it confirmed that Jesus called those things which be not as though they were. Jesus did the same thing his Father did. He took a situation that "was not" and called it as though it were. And, of course, it eventually became what Jesus had already called it.

The fact that this same incident was recorded by three different writers — Mark, Matthew, and Luke — shows us that 1) the people watching this miracle were obviously moved by what they heard and saw, and more importantly, 2) *the Holy Spirit had it recorded three different times to emphasize the importance of this spiritual truth.* It is imperative to say with our mouth what God says.

4.   These things said he: and after that he saith unto them, OUR FRIEND LAZARUS SLEEPETH; but I go, that I may awake him out of sleep.

- John 11:11

When Jesus made this statement, it's important to realize that Lazarus was dead. By Jesus' own admission in verse 14, he said unto them *plainly, "Lazarus is dead."* So, without a doubt, Lazarus had died. But if Lazarus was dead, *and since*

Jesus knew he was dead, why did Jesus say that Lazarus was sleeping?

The answer is obvious. Again, Jesus was calling those things which be not as though they were. Just as God had called it in Genesis 17:5, and just as Jesus had called it with the daughter of Jairus, Jesus was again saying it here with Lazarus. The purpose of calling those things which be not as though they were *is because this is a part of what's involved in changing the circumstances.* In every single instance where something "was not," yet it was called as *though* it were, you'll notice that the circumstance was changed.

When Jesus later arrived at the tomb, he said in verse 41, *"Father, I thank thee that thou HAST (past tense) heard me,"* **even though Lazarus was still in the tomb**. Obviously, Jesus believed that God had already answered his prayer. In fact, in the previous verse Jesus said, *"Said I not unto thee, that, if thou wouldest believe, thou shouldest see the glory of God?"* Notice the order — 1) if thou wouldest believe, then 2) thou shouldest see. Seeing does not come before believing. Believing always comes before seeing. Or it could be said, seeing always follows believing. This is the faith that pleases God — we first believe, then see.

5.   And, behold, there was a woman which had a spirit of infirmity eighteen years, and was bowed together, and could in no wise lift up herself. And when Jesus saw her, he called her to him, and SAID unto her, woman, THOU ARE LOOSED FROM THINE INFIRMITY.
- Luke 13:11-12

When Jesus said that this woman was loosed from her infirmity, to anyone staring at her they would have thought, *"How can Jesus say that she's loosed when it's so obviously apparent that she isn't loosed?"* There's no doubt that she was still bowed over, in the same condition that she had been for the past 18 years. She didn't look any different.

But Jesus lived in a different realm. He lived in the realm of faith. Faith is only moved by what it believes, not by what it sees. Jesus recognized the fact that this woman was still bowed over, but he was in the process of changing the facts. He was calling those things which be not as though they were. Then he laid his hands on her:

And he laid his hands on her: and immediately she was made straight, and glorified God.

- Luke 13:13

You notice that Jesus didn't first lay his hands on her, heal her, and then say, *"Woman, you are loosed from your infirmity."* No, he said that she was loosed from her infirmity *before* her back was made straight. This is where many people miss it. They don't want to say that they're healed until after they feel or look better. They have the order mixed up. We say with our mouth what we believe *first*, then it becomes what we were saying and believing. This woman eventually got to straighten up, *but not until after Jesus said that she was already loosed from her infirmity*.

Summary

Every child in Sunday School is taught to be like Jesus. A

common question which has even been printed into bumper stickers and wristbands is, *"What would Jesus do?"* The ultimate example in life is Jesus. He lived the lifestyle in word and deed that we should follow. Why then should it seem strange to call those things which be not as though they were when we're just following in the footsteps of our Lord? Abraham was just acting like God when he did it, and we're just acting like Jesus when we do it. We're not denying reality, we're changing reality.

The life of faith is the most exciting lifestyle that there is. People who don't understand faith won't understand you. With Jesus in Matthew's account we saw that the people ridiculed what he said. We shouldn't find it surprising then that people may react to us with an upraised eyebrow. But people of faith are concerned about pleasing God and changing circumstances.

Everything in this world is programmed to expect the worst. And, to be honest, bad things are continually happening in this world. We're not denying that. It's just that we're putting our foot down and denying bad circumstances the ability to dominate us. Instead of circumstances controlling us, we're controlling circumstances. We call those things which be not as though they were because we're shaping our lives around what we believe which, in turn, is based on what God says in His Word. We're allowing what Jesus bought for us in His death, burial, and resurrection to dominate our thinking, believing, speaking, and living.

SECTION 3

STANDING

CHAPTER 10

STANDING
(RECOGNIZING THE STRATEGIES OF THE DEVIL)

PART 1

But let him ask in faith, NOTHING WAVERING...
- James 1:6

If one preaches receiving without standing, people tend to give up before the manifestation of their prayer has an opportunity to come to pass. If one preaches on standing, then people tend to divert their faith from when they pray to some time out in the distant future. Their faith then is mistakenly changed to hope.

The key is, as Jesus said, to believe that we receive it when we pray. The manifestation will be forthcoming, but our responsibility is to continue to believe. Always remember, the manifestation of our answer is simply the byproduct of our believing. If we have this understanding, we can approach the subject of standing correctly in a positive manner.

Notice again:

But let him ask in faith, NOTHING WAVERING...
- James 1:6

The fact that we're told not to waver shows us that we're going to have opportunities to waver once we pray. For if the manifestation of every answer came to pass immediately, the apostle James wouldn't have written the above verse. The fact that we're told not to waver shows us that we need to know something about how to stand in the face of seemingly unanswered prayer.

Of course, we believe that our prayer _was_ answered when we prayed, but some things take some time to come to pass, especially so in financial matters. It's from this time that we say *"Amen"* to the time when our answer is physically manifest that we need to have an understanding of how the devil operates. The devil would like nothing more than to keep us from using our faith. If he can get us to unwittingly stop believing, he will have considered it a success.

Always remember, the devil didn't have the ability to keep us from getting born again when we made Jesus the Lord of our life. He also didn't have the ability to keep us from receiving the baptism of the Holy Spirit. He likewise doesn't have the ability to keep our answers in prayer from coming to pass if we continue to believe during and after we pray.

His primary weapon is deceit and trickery _in our minds_. He works in our minds by injecting _thoughts_ of doubt. He tries to make us doubt our salvation. He tries to make us doubt our infilling of the Holy Spirit. He tries to make us doubt any answer to prayer. If we learn to recognize these attacks in our thought-life as being from the devil, there won't be any demonic force that can keep us from receiving or losing our answers in prayer. This is a vital area of understanding that needs to addressed. We must be able to recognize the workings and strategies of the devil and demonic forces.

1) **The devil has the ability to put thoughts into our minds and to make it appear that his thoughts are our thoughts.**

Background Information: **From that time forth began Jesus to show unto his disciples, how that he must go unto Jerusalem, and suffer many things of the elders and chief priests and scribes, and be killed, and be raised again the third day.**
- Matthew 16:21

Here we have positive proof that Jesus had taught the disciples about his death, burial, and resurrection. Jesus took the time *ahead of time* to prepare them for what was going to happen those 3 days and nights. Had the disciples understood his teaching they would've been saved all the anguish they went through during that time. But notice what Peter said:

Then Peter took him, and began to rebuke him (Jesus), saying, Be it far from thee, Lord: this shall not be unto thee. But he (Jesus) turned, and _said unto Peter_, Get thee behind me, Satan...
- Matthew 16:22-23

When Peter heard Jesus say that he was going to be killed, Peter rebuked Jesus and began to *reason* with Jesus. He said, *"No Jesus. Nothing like that will happen to you."* But then Jesus turned and said to Peter, *"Get thee behind me Satan."* Of course, Jesus wasn't calling Peter Satan. We see here that Peter's thinking processes were unknowingly being **led** *by Satan.* Peter didn't realize the thoughts that were in his mind were put into his mind by the devil. He thought that _he_ was just thinking those thoughts.

This shows us that the devil has the ability to put his thoughts into people's minds and, from all appearances, it seems that _we_ are just thinking those thoughts. He makes it to *appear* that we're just thinking those thoughts. In other words, our minds are able to receive thoughts from the evil spirit world. The devil and demons *continually* try to put thoughts into our minds.

Most people don't realize this, anymore than Peter realized this. If Peter would have realized that his thinking processes at the moment were the thoughts of the devil he would have rejected it immediately, just like most people today would reject it. Most people think that it's *just them* thinking those thoughts.

This is why it's absolutely imperative that we renew our minds with the Word of God (Romans 12:2). We have to be able to distinguish between what is God and what is the devil. There are a thousand-and-one things in the world that are trying to get our attention every hour of every day. *More importantly, the devil will try to lead our thought-life if we're unaware of it,* and the whole time we'll think that it's just us thinking those thoughts.

2) The Battleground Is The Mind

In whom the god of this world (the devil) hath blinded THE MINDS of them which believe not, lest the light of the glorious gospel of Christ, who is the image of God, should shine unto them.
- 2 Corinthians 4:4

In this verse we see that the devil works at blinding *the minds* of unbelievers to keep them from seeing the light of the glorious gospel. Of course, this also reveals how the devil works in the lives of believers as well. The devil tries to blind *the minds* of believers from seeing *further* light of the glorious gospel. We know that this is true, because there are thousands of churches that disagree with each other over certain Bible truths. They're all sincere, but some churches are blinded from certain truths that other churches are enjoying.

Again, the devil works in people's minds. *Your* mind is what the devil wants to try to get hold of. If more Christians realized this, they wouldn't do and say a lot of the things that they're doing and saying. They would keep their minds in check, and as a result, they would keep their bodies and tongues in check. Notice again:

In whom the god of this world hath blinded *the minds*...
- 2 Corinthians 4:4

107

The mind is the battleground. If more Christians would get hold of this it would completely turn their lives around. *The entrance to the heart is through the mind.* So what the devil tries to do is to confuse us in our minds. For example, Peter wasn't willingly or purposely trying to yield to the thoughts of the devil. He was sincerely trying to think of what was best for Jesus and him. *He was reasoning*.

This is one of the arenas in life in which we have to be very careful. The devil can *reason* you out of your healing. He can *reason* you out of the baptism of the Holy Spirit. Reasoning apart from God and his Word is very dangerous.

CHAPTER 11

STANDING
(RECOGNIZING THE STRATEGIES OF THE DEVIL)

PART 2

3) We must forcefully control our thought life.

> _Casting down imaginations_, and every high thing that exalteth itself against the knowledge of God, _and bringing into captivity every thought_ to the obedience of Christ.
> **- 2 Corinthians 10:5**

We are to purposely control our thought life. The reason, as we saw in the preceding chapter, is because the devil will try to inject his thoughts into our minds. If we're not actively watching and leading our every thought, the devil will try to get some weeds, so to speak, into our minds to choke out the good thoughts.

Thoughts are continually coming to our minds. We obviously can't keep thoughts from coming, *but we can decide what stays in our minds*. EVERY NEW, UNFAMIL-IAR THOUGHT MUST BE EXAMINED AND SCRUTI-NIZED. A decision has to be made on whether or not it should be allowed to stay in our thinking. Should that new, unfamiliar thought turn out to be opposed to the knowledge of God (the Word of God), it must be ejected.

Any thought that the devil tries to put into our minds must forcefully be removed. They cannot be allowed to aimlessly float around in our thinking every so often. If that happens, it will come back to haunt us sooner or later. The moment that we realize it's of the devil these thought must be brought into captivity and then cast down.

Difference Between "Letting Go" And "Casting Down"

There is a difference between "letting something go" and "casting something down." In fact, the very nature of the phrase "casting down" implies something that is done with force. You see, if we "let something go," we are *releasing* something. But if we "cast something down," we are *forcefully ejecting* something.

For example, if we "let" the dog out, we're saying that the dog is again welcome back sometime. If we "kick" the dog out, we're saying that we don't ever want to see the dog again! This is exactly what we have to do with the thoughts that the devil tries to bring to our minds. We don't just "let"

110

these thoughts go, we bring them into captivity. That is, we don't allow them to stay free in our thinking, then we expel them. In short, we reject them to eject them.

Since we're in a warfare (2 Cor. 10:4-5) we must guard and protect our minds. If a doubt about our healing comes to mind, we must deal with it immediately. *We do not tolerate one thought contrary to our healing for one second.* The longer we dwell on the doubts, the more of a foothold the devil will try to establish in our thinking. This is how the devil builds strongholds in people's minds.

The Devil Is Persistent

And when the devil had ended all the temptation, he departed from him FOR A SEASON.
- Luke 4:13

Contrary to most people's understanding, the three temptations that Jesus faced on the mount were not the only encounter that Jesus had with the devil in his ministry. This verse plainly states that the devil departed from Jesus *for a season*. In other words, the devil was out to get at Jesus any place that he could find it. We saw it in Matthew 16. The devil tried to get to Jesus through Peter's thinking.

Notice how the Amplified Bible reads this verse:

...he (the devil) left him — temporarily, that is, stood off from Him *until another more opportune and favorable time*.

111

This is how the devil operates. He looks for situations that he considers "favorable opportunities," moments where he thinks you'll be the weakest. Because God expects us to operate by faith and not by sight, the devil will try to influence us to operate by sight instead of by faith. After prayer, he says, *"Do you feel better? Do you look any better? Do you have the money in your hands?"*

We have to realize that these thoughts are not *our* thoughts. *This is where the battle takes place.* If the devil can convince you that you didn't receive your healing when you prayed, you'll lose it before it has the opportunity to come to pass. Once you've prayed, you cannot tolerate for one second any thought that is contrary to your healing. Your body is no longer the battleground at this point. *Your mind is!* Your body is simply the spoils of the victor for whoever wins. If the devil wins, your body will stay sick. If you win, your healing will come to pass.

Our responsibility is to develop a dogged perseverence. Every time a thought comes to our mind that says we didn't receive our healing, we have to rise up and resist. We cannot allow that thought to stay free in our thinking. We have to capture it. We say, *"No, I resist that doubt. I rebuke that lie. I believe that I received my healing in Jesus' name."*

Casting Down Reasonings

As we saw with Peter, many times the lies from the devil come as reasonings in our minds. In fact, the Amplified Bible translates 2 Corinthians 10:5 as, *"Casting down reasonings..."*.

112

For example, the thoughts could come something like this — *"Hmm, it's been awhile since I was prayed for. And to be honest, I don't feel any different. I can't tell that I'm any better. I know it's the will of God that I be healed, but since I didn't receive my healing this time, I know I will the next time."*

Doesn't that sound good? The reasoning is that it's still the will of God for this person to be healed. But because he couldn't feel any difference in his body, he figured he didn't receive it that time, but he's sure he will the next time. This kind of reasoning is sincere. It *sounds* right, but it's a lie from demonic forces. The battle for that person's healing was won by the devil. Why? Because the healing was left relegated to some unknown future date. This person's healing, which could have been won right then, was lost for the time being.

Faith Is Now

You see, faith is now. If it's not now, it's not faith. The devil could care less just because we admit that healing is the will of God. We could say that healing is for all of God's children (which it is), but we didn't say anything that the devil didn't already know. He's known for 6,000 years that God wants his people to be blessed. We haven't ruffled his feathers one bit, so to speak.

But it bothers him greatly when we declare our healing in the midst of pain and physical discomfort. When we say, *"I believe that I receive my healing right now. I don't care how I feel. I don't care how I look. I believe that I'm healed now in Jesus' name,"* now we've said something that the devil is

113

afraid of. Of course, the devil will now bring thoughts to our minds that are contrary to what we say we believe. The thoughts will say, *"You're not healed. Feel, look, see, touch. If you were healed you would feel better. If you were healed you would look better. If you were healed you wouldn't be in pain. Sure, healing is the will of God, but you didn't receive it then. Next time you'll receive it. The next time it will work out. But you're not healed now."*

But we have to affirm in faith, *"I don't care what thoughts come to my mind that are contrary to my healing. I forget about the future. I forget about the next time. In fact, why do I even need to think about the next time? I believe I'm healed right now."*

That is faith. Faith is now. We scare the devil, so to speak, when we say, *"Now I've got it."* You see, the devil wants us to operate by sight, and God wants us to operate by faith. At the moment we may not look it or feel it, but our job is to walk by what we believe we've received, not by what we see.

The reason this needs to be taught is because we need to realize that there is a fight to faith. Some people have the mistaken idea that if they walk by faith, then everything is going to be easy. They assume that if things should ever get difficult they must have missed God, or they must have slipped and somehow stopped walking by faith. *That's not true.*

I want to assure you that nothing is wrong. Actually, everything is more than right. The battle has begun. Contrary thoughts wouldn't be coming to your mind a hundred times a minute if you hadn't made the move to possess the land.

The Fight Of Faith

Fight the good *fight* of faith...
1 Timothy 6:12

You notice that Paul didn't say to *coast* the easy *coast* of faith. In this verse the Holy Spirit is emphasizing a different aspect of faith. It's important to realize that faith is a *fight*. It's going contrary to this world system and against all that the world teaches. *More importantly, it is directly opposing everything that the devil has spent years trying to build.* This is why when we make a claim by faith contrary thoughts immediately come to our minds.

Faith may not be easy initially, but it's rewarding a thousand times over. When the leukemia in your body has completely vanished, what does it matter that you had an uphill fight? When the sugar in your blood registers normal and you no longer have to inject insulin into your body, what does it matter what you had to go through to get it? When the cancerous tumor in your liver has completely dissipated, what does it matter that you had a faith-fight to face? Thank God, you're healed!

Labor To Enter

Hebrews 4:11 says to labor to enter into rest. You see, rest is the goal, but we have to labor to enter into it. We have to buck the downstream thinking that the devil has sold this world. We have to make a 180 degree turn in our thinking and go upstream. It's something that we have to work at, to struggle for. It's *labor*. Sometimes it's *difficult* labor. The devil is fighting to keep every inch that we're trying to gain.

When the thoughts of doubt come, what are we going to do about it? Should we cave into them and float down the current of life like a dead piece of wood? Or are we going to buck the devil's thoughts and keep believing God? I'll tell you what we're going to do, we're going to buck the devil's thoughts and keep believing God. We're going to stay in the fight of faith and labor to enter into rest.

When the diabetes is gone, when the leukemia is gone, when the tumor is gone, it's worth it. When our healing has come to pass and our health has sprung forth, it's worth it. When our prosperity comes to pass, it's worth it. When the mortgage is paid off, when the new cars sitting in the garage are paid off, when the refrigerator and pantry is full, it's worth it. When the smoke has cleared in our mind and the battle is over, and we have in our hands that which we greatly desired, there's no better euphoria of knowing that we got what the devil said was impossible to obtain.

The Good Fight Of Faith

Paul told Timothy to fight. Not to fight with *people* or to fight with the *devil*, but to fight the *fight of faith*. The arena that we're to get into is the **_arena of faith_**. If we get into any other arena, the devil will defeat us every single time. But if we refuse to budge from the arena of faith, we'll defeat the devil every single time. This is why Paul said it's the *good* fight of faith. Notice again:

Fight the GOOD fight of faith...
- 1 Timothy 6:12

The reason the fight of faith is good is because it's the one fight that we can win every single time. There's not any other fight in the Bible that we are commanded to fight except the fight of faith. This is why some Christians end up getting hurt. They're trying to fight the devil on *his* turf, in *his* arena. Don't allow you to get suckered into any other fight except the fight *of faith*. When we fight the fight of faith, we are wrestling against principalities and powers who are trying to get us to stop our stand of faith. Let's keep the devil on <u>our</u> terms, in the arena that God has told <u>us</u> to fight in. As far as we are concerned, this is the only fight that is a good fight.

Don't let the word "good" confuse you. <u>*Good does not*</u> <u>*mean easy.*</u> You notice that Paul said it is still a fight. The very nature of the word "fight" means *"a conflict or struggle."* In his next letter to Timothy, Paul said to endure <u>*hardness*</u> as a good soldier of Jesus Christ (2 Timothy 2:3). Thank God, the word "good" does mean it's a fight that we can win.

The spoils of the victory is our healing. It's our prosperity, etc. It's the *rest* that God has promised us. These spoils have been God-ordained that we partake of them. Wherever the soles of our feet shall tread in the promised land of healing and prosperity, God has given them to us.

Summary

The mind is the target area of the devil. *The devil seeks to influence people's minds through trickery, deceit, confusion, and outright lies*. If we fail to recognize his tactics, we'll be on an up-and-down emotional roller coaster. One minute we'll say, *"I believe I've got it,"* the next minute we'll say, *"I wonder if I really have it."* In effect, we're being double-minded. One minute we're standing, another minute we're yielding to the doubts that the devil brings to our minds. Notice the disastrous results that James says this kind of thinking leaves us in:

...*nothing wavering*. For he that wavereth is like a wave of the sea driven with the wind and tossed. *For let not that man think that he shall receive any thing of the Lord*. A double-minded man is unstable in all his ways.
- James 1:6-8

We cannot be double-minded. We cannot allow us to waver. If we've prayed for healing, we don't say that we're healed one minute, and then say that we're not healed the next minute. As James said, *"...let not that man think that he shall receive any thing of the Lord."* We must recognize the thoughts that the devil tries to bring to our minds and cast them down. Our minds were designed by God to work in harmony with our hearts.

The good news is, we don't have to be deceived, and we don't have to be confused. We have the correct information, and the ability given to us by God to withstand these attacks in our minds. The key is to remain constant in our minds and in our words through thick-and-thin. Notice:

Let us hold fast the profession (confession) of our faith WITHOUT WAVERING...
- Hebrews 10:23

Let us hold fast to saying the same thing, regardless of the ever-changing feelings of the body or circumstances. The secret is in learning *not to yield* to the thoughts that the devil brings to our minds.

When I say to be constant in our minds, I'm not saying that we won't have any thoughts of doubt come to our minds. By virtue of the fact that the mind is the battleground means that this is where the devil is going to attack. Thus, contrary and conflicting thoughts *will* come to our minds *and sometimes persist in trying to stay*. Just because we find conflicting thoughts in our minds it doesn't mean that these thoughts are *our* thoughts. Faith in our heart will work with this intruder of doubt in our head.

The key is to recognize these thoughts as being from the devil and not yielding to them. This is why God has given us his Word. It's our road-map, so to speak, through sickness, financial distress, and every crisis of life. When wrong thoughts come to our minds, we are to stick with what the Word of God says.

Thou wilt keep him in perfect peace *whose mind is stayed on thee*: **because he** *trusteth* **(has faith) in thee.**
- Isaiah 26:3

119

Victory comes when we're using the faith in our heart and keeping our mind constant on God's Word through the storms of life.

CHAPTER 12

STANDING
(WHAT TO DO WHILE FAITH IS GROWING)

PART 3

There is another aspect of standing that is equally important. Many people who pray the prayer of faith do not have their faith sufficiently developed to receive whatever it is that they desire of the Lord. Yes, it is the will of God that they possess the promise, but their faith is not strong enough to appropriate the promise.

Of course, their faith can grow, and should grow so that they can obtain. The reason some people need to stand is because they need to allow their faith the necessary time to grow and develop. This is a spiritual law that is seen throughout the scriptures. What we use is strengthened, what we fail to use is weakened. Thus, for faith to grow, we must use it.

The following scriptures reveal that there are different developments of faith:

weak faith	Romans 4:19
strong faith	Romans 4:20
little faith	Matthew 14:31
great faith	Matthew 8:10
exceedingly growing faith	2 Thessalonians 1:3

Clearly then, faith grows. We all start out with the measure of faith (Romans 12:3) when we make Jesus the Lord of our life. What we do with this measure of faith afterwards is up to us. *We* are the ones responsible for feeding and exercising our faith upon God's Word to see that it grows and develops.

According to 2 Corinthians 1:20, *all* the promises of God are the will of God for everyone of His children. *But our faith has a part to play in whether or not these promises are able to come to pass in our lives*. Take, for example, Abraham:

He (Abraham) staggered not at the promise of God through unbelief; but was STRONG in faith...
- Romans 4:20

You notice that this scripture states that Abraham was strong in faith. In order for his faith to have been strong, it obviously, at one time, had to have grown to be strong. The following translations bring out this fact more clearly:

No unbelief or distrust made him waver or doubtingly question concerning the promise of God, but

he GREW STRONG and was empowered by faith...
> - Amplified Bible

Yet he did not waver through unbelief regarding the promise of God, but was STRENGTHENED IN HIS FAITH...
> - New International Version

But Abraham never doubted. He believed God, FOR HIS FAITH AND TRUST GREW EVER STRONGER...
> - Living Bible (Paraphrase)

...yet with respect to the promise of God, he did not waver in unbelief, but GREW STRONG IN FAITH...
> - New American Standard Bible

It's clear that Abraham's faith grew. He didn't start out as a faith-giant, so to speak, but his faith grew to make him a faith-giant. Abraham had a lot of ups and downs, he made a lot of mistakes, and he faced many insurmountable obstacles. *He overcame them all and is today considered the father of our faith.*

This is where many people miss it. Many don't have the patience to allow them the time to grow and develop. Once they pray, if they don't feel any better, or if things don't look any better immediately, they want to quit and give up.

Spiritual development, like physical development, takes time and exercise. I have yet to see a high school football player go directly to the NFL. I haven't seen a junior-high basketball player become the center for the Boston Celtics. They're just not able. They have the heart and zeal, but they don't have the experience and the physical capabilities.

Likewise, spiritually speaking, heart and zeal are necessary prerequisites, *but heart and zeal alone are not enough*. It takes spiritual development. Many young or underdeveloped Christians want to completely ignore boot camp and jump to the front lines. When the pressure becomes too much for them, they get blown away and we never hear from them again. Others, because of a lack of sound teaching do ignorant things. Some people jump out of the foxholes of medicine, so to speak, before they're ready. Others jump out of the planes of financial blessing before they have their parachutes of tithing and offerings secure. The point is, faith needs to be developed. It doesn't happen overnight.

Like Peter in Matthew chapter 14, to begin the journey of faith, we all have to step onto the water sometime. Some of us may go under immediately. Some of us, like Peter, may stay up for a little bit, but then gradually sink. If and when we start to go under, *don't be condemned if you have to get back into the boat*.

You're not going to prove anything to anyone just aimlessly floating around in the sea during a storm. *If the boat is there, use it*. Don't allow you to feel guilty about failing. Hey, at least you got out of the boat! The other 11 stayed in the boat and didn't even try. You actually attempted to use your faith. This is how faith grows — by using it.

Of course, there is such a thing as overextending our faith.

Faith 3 — While Faith Is Growing

If I was a weightlifter and couldn't lift 120 pounds, I'm certainly not going to be able to lift 450 pounds. *I'll never develop my muscles if all I ever do is try to lift 450 pounds.* Muscles cannot develop by being continually _over_extended. Muscles grow by being _fully_-extended. Only as we consistently practice lifting what we're capable of lifting do our muscles develop to the point that we can lift more.

Faith is the same. Before we can successfully face the Goliath's of life we must first be able to overcome the lions and bears of life. Before we try to walk on the water in a storm, we must first ride in a boat in a storm. Before we tackle the mountains, we must first be able to handle the fig trees. Before we can believe God against cancer, we must first be able to believe God against a migraine.

Of course, this is the ideal situation, but this is not always possible. The person who has cancer and just now hears the message of faith doesn't have the time to practice. He's immediately thrown into a heavyweight fight without any preparation. His life is on the line.

Sadly, I've heard some moronic people tell these people who are reaching out for a miracle that if they're going to use their faith, then they can't use any medicine. It's amazing that a person would tell a sick person such a thing. The thing is, if you don't want to use any medicine that is between you and God. _You definitely don't have the right to tell someone else if they can or cannot use any medicine_.

That would be like telling Peter that he couldn't get back into the boat. Fortunately, Jesus didn't have that kind of an attitude. Since Peter didn't have the developed faith to remain on the water, Jesus led him back to the boat. If your faith isn't sufficiently developed to appropriate your healing, then get into the boat of medical science. At least you won't go under and drown.

Jesus didn't have a problem with helping Peter back into the boat, and he doesn't have a problem with you using medicinal aids to get out of the sea of disease. It wouldn't have done the church any good if Peter would have drowned in the sea that day. By giving him more time to sit under the teaching ministry of Jesus, his faith was able to grow. Look at what happened a year or two later because of his faith.

Don't ever let anyone put you under condemnation if you need medicine to keep you well or to keep you alive. If you need chemotherapy, and if it can help you, then don't hesitate to be treated. If radiation can help, then use it. If glycerine can keep your heart beating, take it.

My goodness, we're talking about your life here! Who cares what some overzealous quack says. He may be sincere, but he's sincerely wrong. I thank God for all that faith can accomplish, but if your faith is not developed to the degree to bring your healing to pass, then do what you have to do to live. Staying alive is more important than some ridiculous pride in not using medicine.

Besides, why not let the two work together? Of course, receiving healing by simply exercising faith in God's Word without the help of medical science is God's best, but the person with a terminal illness who just now hears this mes-

126

sage of faith isn't in a position to respond in such a way as to appropriate their healing on their own faith. They might receive their healing through the *"gifts of healing"* from a miracle-type ministry where God, for whatever reason, faith or no faith, heals certain people. I enjoy seeing this happen and always look forward to seeing more and more. But if this doesn't happen, we have to be realistic while we're developing our faith.

Medicine Can Be Used Alongside Faith

While our faith is developing, there is absolutely nothing wrong with using medicine. I personally know of two cases where two persons were diagnosed with tumors. They had x-rays, and in one case, had an x-ray, ultra-sound, and a cat-scan. They both immediately started using their faith as best as they knew how.

To make a long story short, because of the seriousness of the cases, they both decided to go through with their operations while they were exercising their faith. Amazingly, when the doctors got inside, the tumors had completely disappeared. Of course, it may not have been God's best to have a permanent scar on their body, but it sure beats losing some needed body parts.

I have a friend who was diagnosed with cancer several years ago. He, too, immediately started using his faith. It was a life-and-death struggle and his life was hanging in the balance. He stretched his faith as far as he could stretch it and decided to have chemotherapy for this cancer. After the first treatment he lost his hair, but are you ready for this? The cancer had completely disappeared. Again, supernatural intervention. Say what you will, but it sure beats dying.

While our faith is growing God is more than pleased to work through doctors and medicine. Medicine doesn't hinder the power of God. For some reason, some people have the idea that if they're taking medicine then they can't use their faith. Or if they're using their faith then they can't take medicine. This is ridiculous.

If you're only using medicine and not using your faith, then you're leaving God out of the healing process. Or if you're using your faith and not using medicine, but if your faith isn't sufficiently developed to bring your healing to pass, then you're suffering in your body needlessly.

Medicine Can Buy You Time

Sometimes medicine can help you to regroup so that you can have some time to pull together, so to speak, and get into a position to exercise your faith. For example, my wife and I know a woman who, several years ago, had a severe and constant pain in her stomach. As the pain continued to increase she went to a doctor. It turned out that she had an ulcer in her stomach. She was prescribed some medicine and was told to change her diet.

She knew it was the will of God for her to be healed. She had an understanding of the scriptures concerning healing that was provided in the atonement 2,000 years ago, *but she also knew that she wasn't ready to pray*.

Hasty Prayer Is Sometimes Ineffective

For instance, recall the man in Mark chapter 9 who had the son who often fell into the water and fire. In desperation the father came to Jesus for help. He said, *"Lord, if you can do anything, please help us"* (verse 22). Jesus immediately turned the whole situation back to this man. In effect, Jesus replied, *"It's not a matter of what I can do, it's a matter of how much you can believe. All things are possible to him that believeth"* (verse 23). You see, it's *our* responsibility to exercise faith.

Our woman friend knew that she needed some time to get into a position to release her faith. Sometimes I think that we rush into prayer without any preparation. It's not beneficial to hastily or flippantly mutter a prayer without thinking about what we're doing. Sometimes it may be necessary to meditate on the particular scriptures that cover our need. Sometimes we may need to search our heart to see if we have any unforgiveness toward our brethren. It's not a matter of what God can do. The situation calls for *us* to release *our* faith. It's the degree of faith that is released that allows God the amount that He's able to work.

For the next several days our friend restudied the scriptures on healing. The evening of the fourth day we prayed. She believed that she received her healing for that ulcerated stomach. She said, *"I believe that my stomach is now healed."*

When she woke up the next morning the normal pain that accompanied that ulcer was completely gone. From that day forward she never needed another dose of medicine. At the time of this writing, that happened almost 18 years ago and she has been healed ever since.

Now, the question is, did that medication heal her ulcer? Of course not. What the medicine did during those 4 days is that it allowed her some temporary relief from the pain while she was getting into a position to release her faith. So then, medicine can give you time to regroup and give you some time to reread and restudy the scriptures in your particular area of need. Or, it can be used at the same time that you're using your faith. If the manifestation of your healing is slow in coming, the medicine can deal with the symptoms while you're exercising your faith until your healing comes to pass. The point is, medicine doesn't hinder healing. Whatever level your faith is at, God just wants it to grow.

Being Fully Persuaded Is
What Produces Results

People who are just beginning to use their faith have to learn the basic principles of faith. For example, when they pray, they may not really believe that they receive their healing, but they **_want_** to believe. They realize that the words of Jesus in Mark 11:24 are true, but they're just starting to act on this verse with a real problem. They're saying that they believe they're healed, but they're not yet quite _fully_ persuaded of their healing (Romans 4:21). This is okay. This is exactly how faith grows. Again, faith grows by using what faith we have.

This is why it's best to develop our faith on situations that are not life-threatening. If you catch a cold, use your faith. If you get a headache, use your faith. Exercise your faith like a weightlifter exercises his muscles. Start with something that is feasible. Realize now, ahead of time, that initially, it's going to be work. When your sinuses are clogged, your head is pounding, and your body feels like it's been put through the wringer, your body isn't going to want you to use any faith. It's going to say, *"Shut the blinds, give me a pill, and leave me alone."* But a headache or a cold isn't life-threatening. This is the perfect opportunity to leave the aspirin in the cabinet and develop your faith.

Develop your faith now. Don't wait until a crisis to try to develop your faith. In the meantime, if your body needs medicine, USE IT. Don't allow you to be condemned by the devil or some misguided person. You're not going to stand before them on the judgement day. You just keep studying the Word of God, and He'll lead you step by step. Just as Jesus helped Peter in Matthew 14, he'll help you. The only thing that matters is that you're on the road to growing faith.

(For more information of medicine, faith, and healing, see my book, UNTANGLING THE HEALING CRISIS, Section 4, chapters 17 through 21.)

CHAPTER 13

HOLD FAST YOUR CONFESSION

Let us hold fast the profession (confession) of our faith without wavering; (for he is faithful that promised;)
- Hebrews 10:23

The fact that we're told to hold fast to the confession of our faith shows us that the answers to our prayers will not be immediately apparent. If the answer was immediately apparent there would not be a need to hold fast to the confession of our faith. The writer wouldn't need to remind us that God is faithful.

Generally, from the time that we say "Amen" until our answer is physically manifest, we're going to have opportunities to give up. Even though it's the will of God for us to obtain the promises, if we don't hold fast to the confession of our faith, the promise that we're standing on will never come to pass. It's extremely important that we refuse to waver from our faith.

Notice again:

Let us hold fast the confession of our faith WITHOUT WAVERING...

Evidently, if we do waver we won't receive our desire. As the apostle James said, *"Let not that man who wavers think that he shall receive anything of the Lord"* (James 1:6-7). One time someone asked, *"How do I not waver?"* The answer is simple — By staying constant, by staying the same. So what are we to stay constant with? Or what are we not to waver from? Notice:

Let us hold fast the CONFESSION OF OUR FAITH without wavering...

As you can see, we're not to waver from the *confession of our faith*. That is, we're to remain constant with *the words that we speak*. If we believe that we've received our answer, we are to continually *say* that. We're to continually say, *"I believe that I've got it."* We shouldn't waver from our confession. For example, if we say, *"I believe that I've got it,"* but then another time say, *"I don't think I've got it,"* we haven't stayed constant with the confession of our faith. As a result, we won't obtain the answer to our prayer, even though God wants us to have it.

To obtain the answer to our prayers this scripture makes it clear that we're to *hold fast* to the confession of our faith in he face of opposing circumstances. What does this mean? The word "hold" means, *"to possess, a grip."* The word "fast" means, *"to bind, to tighten, to clinch."* When these words are combined, this phrase means, *"to possess tightly, a secured grip."* Thus, Hebrews 10:23 is saying:

Let us keep a secure grip on the confession of our faith without budging an inch on what we're saying.

The main object in this verse is the *confession* of our faith. We're to hold fast to it, that is, we're not to waver from it. As we've already noted in earlier chapters, faith is believing *and speaking*. We're to hold fast to the speaking of our faith in the midst of contradictory circumstances. For example, three chapters later, the writer of Hebrews says:

...for he (Jesus) hath said, I will never leave thee, nor forsake thee. So that _we_ may boldly _say_, The Lord is my helper...
- Hebrews 13:5-6

In other words, because God has said that he will never leave us or forsake us, we're to say, *"The Lord is my helper."* Yet when problems arise most people say just the opposite. They say, *"What am I going to do? How am I going to make it? I feel as if the Lord has forsaken me. Where's God when I need him? I don't feel as if God is doing anything."*

You see, they're not saying what the Word of God says to say. But people say, *"But I don't feel like He's with me."* Obviously then, *you can't trust your feelings*. If Jesus said that he would never leave us nor forsake us, *then it's true regardless of what you may or may not feel!* FEELINGS CANNOT BE DEPENDED ON. HIS WORD IS TO BE DEPENDED ON. Regardless of how we may feel, Jesus said that he is with us. It's because of this fact that when circumstances aren't going our way, we need to say that the Lord is our helper. In fact, we're not to just say that, we are to boldly say that.

So that we may BOLDLY SAY, The Lord is my helper...

When we say what the Word of God says because we believe it in our heart this is called the confession of our faith. As Hebrews 10:23 brings out, this confession of faith isn't a one-time thing that we say. It's something that we're to hold fast to, something that we're not to waver from saying. In other words, we're to continually say what the Word of God says — when times are going good *and* when times are going bad. By holding fast to our confession of faith, this will, sooner or later, cause the bad to become good. It takes patience on our part to allow our faith to work.

Here's why we're to hold fast to our confession:

That ye be not slothful, but followers of them who through faith AND PATIENCE inherit the promises.
- Hebrews 6:12

You notice that it's not just faith *alone* that inherits the promises. Though faith is the necessary prerequisite, sometimes, for whatever the reason, faith needs time to work to bring the promise to pass. I think it's important to note that the word "patience" is a little misleading in our modern vernacular. A better word would be "perseverance." — "Who through faith *and perseverance* inherit the promises."

136

We must persevere with our faith. The temptation to give up can, at times, be very strong. This is why we need examples to follow.

That ye be...*followers of them* who through faith and patience inherit the promises.

Who is this "them" that we're to follow? Those who have inherited the promises.

Follow Those Who Obtain The Promises

Many times I've heard people say, *"But what about all those who didn't obtain the promise? What about those who didn't get their healing?"* The answer is simple — ***Don't follow them!*** Of course, we're to encourage them and help them as best as we know how, *but they're not to dissuade us from using our faith to inherit the promises*. Clearly, *our examples are to be those who **have** inherited the promises*.

Just as people in the world pick certain people who "made it" in the business world, or in the sports world to be the examples for a generation to follow, we in the church are to follow those who, through faith and perseverance, have inherited the promises. With the many distractions in the world, and with the fiery darts of the enemy coming against the saints, and with the sludge of cults the devil is using trying to confuse the message of faith, it's always refreshing to see another person persevere with his faith and break through the mess in the world and inherit the promises of God. *These are the people who we in the church are to follow*. They, no doubt, have learned many lessons that we can benefit from.

When sickness comes, we're to hold fast to the confession of our faith. If financial troubles come, we must refuse to waver from the confession of our faith. When opposing circumstances arise, we need to keep a secure grip on our confession.

The Word of God *in our mouth* is a powerful thing. In fact, because of the way God has made us, our words are like a rudder on a ship. Whatever it is we're saying will eventually steer our lives in that direction. If we speak doubt, fear, or death our lives will be filled with doubt, fear, and death. If we speak the Word of God, our lives will be filled with the things of God.

When the negative circumstances of life try to take control of our lives, or try to negate the promise we've taken a stand on, we're to hold fast to the confession of our faith. Why? Because we have a great High Priest in Jesus who is faithful to do His part.

> **Seeing then that we have a great high priest, that is passed into the heavens, *let us hold fast our profession (confession)*...**
> **- Hebrews 4:14**

By holding fast to our confession of faith the answer to our prayer will come to pass.

138

SECTION
4

KEY TRUTHS
ABOUT FAITH

CHAPTER
14

FAITH COMES
BY HEARING
(AND UNDERSTANDING)

O ye of LITTLE faith, why reason ye among yourselves because ye have brought no bread? Do ye not yet UNDERSTAND...

- Matthew 16:8-9a

The little faith of the disciples was, according to Jesus, directly correlated to their lack of understanding. Had they understood, Jesus implied that their faith would not have been little. But because they failed to understand, their potential for great faith was hindered. Faith, then, is the result of a comprehension, or a grasping, so to speak, of the Word of God as it's taught or studied. This is confirmed in Romans 10:17:

So then faith cometh by hearing, and hearing by the word of God.

The Greek word translated "hearing" has its root origin in the word that means "to understand." Romans 10:17 isn't saying that faith comes by the auditory exercise of having sounds hit the drum of the ear. If this were the case, every person in every church service where the Word of God is taught would be able to exercise faith. Those of us in pulpit ministries know that this isn't the case. Some people will grasp it while others won't. Romans 10:17 is talking about an *understanding* of the Word of God. Faith comes when we understand, that is, comprehend the Word of God on the particular subject that is taught.

It's noteworthy that Paul said that faith comes by *"hearing, and hearing... "*. If the comma is removed (actually, there's not any punctuation in the Greek manuscript. All punctuation was added at the liberty of the translators.), Romans 10:17 would read as follows — *"faith cometh by hearing and hearing by the Word of God,"* meaning that faith comes by hearing and hearing and hearing and hearing. This implies much study on our part. For most people faith doesn't come by having heard once. Everyone catches on at different speeds. Faith, for some people, comes by hearing once. For other people, faith comes by hearing and hearing. Yet for other people faith comes only after hearing and hearing and hearing and hearing and hearing. The more we hear, the better the opportunity we have to understand. The more we understand, the greater our capacity for faith. Thus, the capacity for faith comes by studying and gaining an understanding of the Word of God.

For example, if we want faith for healing, we should study the many scriptures in God's Word on healing. If it's faith for prosperity, we should study the many scriptures in God's Word on prosperity. If we need wisdom, we study scriptures on wisdom. If it's the family, we study scriptures on the family. Whatever the subject that we want or need to develop our faith in, we need to go to God's Word to find the corresponding scriptures. As we study God's Word in these many different areas the light, so to speak, will come. Sometimes it comes easily, and other times we have to break through some erroneous traditions that have been built into our minds through wrong teaching and it takes longer.

Thus, our potential for faith is in direct correlation to the comprehension that we gain of God's Word. Our faith depends upon knowing the facts as revealed by God in his Word. Faith isn't reaching into some unknown gray area beyond our understanding. Faith is simply our response to a clear understanding of God's Word.

This is why Hosea 4:6 says, *"My people are destroyed for a lack of knowledge."* In other words, faith and knowledge of God's Word are inseparable. We can't have faith without the knowledge of God's Word, and we can't have a revelation of God's Word without it producing faith. If we have an understanding of God's Word, faith is automatically present.

This is why it's a waste of time and effort for people to work themselves up physically or emotionally trying to get into faith. Some people will strain hard by clenching their hands and squinting their eyes trying to have faith. Other people will pray for it. Others will fast for it. But faith doesn't come in this way. Of course, we need to pray and fast. Waiting upon God helps us to be more sensitive to the moving of the Spirit. The point is, faith doesn't come in this way. Faith comes by hearing and hearing by the Word of God. Take salvation for example.

How Faith Came For Salvation

And he showed us how he (Cornelius) had seen an angel in his house, which stood and said unto him, Send men to Joppa, and call for Simon, whose surname is Peter; WHO SHALL TELL THEE WORDS, whereby thou and all thy house shall be saved.
- Acts 11:13-14

Cornelius was a devout man — one who prayed, one who gave substantial gifts of money to the poor, and one who had seen an angel. Yet as wonderful as all of this was, he didn't have faith for salvation. Certainly we need to be sincere, we need to pray, and we should give offerings to the poor. Faith, though, doesn't come this way. The instructions from the angel were clear and simple — Cornelius needed to *HEAR WORDS in order to be saved*. Since we're saved through faith (Ephesians 2:8), and because faith comes by hearing the Word of God, *we must have knowledge of God's Word*. We cannot believe beyond our knowledge of God's Word. Bible information is what caused Cornelius to have faith for salvation.

How Faith Came For Healing

And there they (Paul and Barnabas) PREACHED THE GOSPEL. And there sat a certain man at Lystra, impotent in his feet, being a cripple from his mother's

144

womb, who never had walked: the same HEARD PAUL
SPEAK...

- Acts 14:7-9a

This cripple heard Paul speak, that is, he heard Paul
preaching the gospel. Obviously the gospel that Paul was
preaching was not only salvation but healing as well. As this
cripple was listening to Paul speak about the great redemptive
truths of Christ, he began to comprehend the information that
Paul was preaching. He came to the realization that Christ
came for the purpose of redeeming man spirit, soul, AND
BODY. At this point, Paul took notice of the man:

**(The cripple) heard Paul speak: (And Paul)
steadfastly beholding him AND PERCEIVING THAT HE
HAD FAITH TO BE HEALED, Said with a loud voice,
Stand upright on thy feet. And he leaped and walked.**
- Acts 14:9-10

When this crippled man heard Paul speak, faith came. It's
encouraging to point out that Romans 10:17 says, *"So then
faith cometh..."*. It doesn't say that faith *might* come, faith
always comes with the understanding of God's Word. When
we grasp the Word of God in our heart faith is automatically
there. Had not Paul preached, this crippled man couldn't have
had faith to be healed. But by hearing the Word of God
through Paul's preaching, faith came. Healing was the end
result.

How Faith Comes For The Miraculous

And he said unto them, Go ye into all the world,

145

and PREACH THE GOSPEL to every creature. He that BELIEVETH and is baptized shall be saved; but he that believeth not shall be damned. And these signs shall follow them that BELIEVE; In my name shall they cast out devils, they shall speak with new tongues; They shall take up serpents; and if they drink any deadly thing, it shall not hurt them; they shall lay hands on the sick, and they shall recover.

- Mark 16:15-18

According to Jesus, the opportunity and capability to believe comes as the result of hearing preaching. People can't believe until they're first exposed to the preaching of the gospel. This is the whole purpose for preaching, to give people the capability to believe. Paul put it this way:

How then shall they call on him in whom they have not believed? And how shall they believe in him of whom they have not heard? And how shall they hear without a preacher? ...So then faith cometh by hearing, and hearing by the word of God.

- Romans 10:14, 17

A person can't believe until they hear the Word of God. The purpose for the five-fold ministry gifts (the apostle, prophet, evangelist, pastor, and teacher as listed in Ephesians 4:11-13) is to teach and preach the Word of God. People who avail themselves to such teaching and preaching have the potential to believe. Jesus said that certain miracles would follow those of us who would believe — exercising authority over the devil, speaking with other tongues, and the healing of the sick by the laying on of hands.

146

The prerequisite to the miraculous is the believing, and the prerequisite to the believing is the preaching of the Word of God, with the implication being that those who hear have understood. Again, the order is 1) hearing preaching, then 2) believing.

Further, the Greek word translated "word" in Romans 10:17, *"So then faith cometh by hearing, and hearing by the **WORD** of God,"* is *rhema. Rhema* simply means, *"the spoken word."* As such this verse reads like this, *"So then faith cometh by hearing, and hearing by the **spoken** word of God."*

This confirms what we saw with Cornelius and the crippled man. Cornelius received faith for salvation by hearing Peter teach. The crippled man received faith for healing by hearing Paul preach. This is what Jesus meant in Mark chapter 16 when he said to go into all the world and preach. Why? So that people could believe. Faith comes by hearing the Word of God *spoken* through teaching and preaching.

It's to our advantage to study the Word of God and to sit under proven ministries that teach and preach the Word of God. The development of our faith relies on such study of God's Word. This is how we grow and develop *spiritually.* It's beyond an *intellectual* pursuit of knowledge, though our mental understanding is certainly involved in the processing of Bible data. But faith is of the *spirit.* The writer of Proverbs said it this way — *"Trust in the Lord with ALL THINE HEART, and lean not unto thine own understanding"* (Proverbs 3:5). In other words, there's a difference between an understanding in the heart and an understanding in the in-

147

tellect. Proverbs 3:5 could be written in this way, *"Trust in the Lord with all the understanding in thine heart, and lean not unto thine own intellectual understanding."* Faith, then, is more accurately an understanding of the Word of God in the heart.

When we study God's Word it goes into our mind on its way to our spirit. The Word of God is *spiritually* discerned, yet our mind is the link between the Word of God on paper and the Word of God that's alive in our spirit. As we meditate on the scriptures, it becomes a part of us. Our thinking processes allow our spirit to feed on God's Word much like our body feeds on natural food. In fact, the formula for success that God gave to Joshua was to meditate on God's Word day and night (Joshua 1:8). Obviously, the person who will keep his mental energies focused on thinking about God's Word day and night is the person whose spirit will soar to new heights.

It's vital to keep our mind focused on God's Word. This is how we begin to understand the many truths of God's Word in our heart. As the light begins to dawn on us, meaning we begin to comprehend what God's Word says and means, faith will begin to grow.

The centurion in Matthew chapter 8 had obviously given much time in thought to the healing ministry of Jesus. He evidently had carefully studied His healing the sick because he recognized the authority in which Jesus ministered. He compared it to his own authority from an earthly, natural standpoint. He said, *"I am a man under authority, having soldiers under me: and I say to this man, Go, and he goeth;*

and to another, Come, and he cometh; and to my servant, Do this, and he doeth it. But speak the word only, and my servant shall be healed" (Matthew 8:8-9). This kind of a revelation in the heart comes only after much deliberate meditation. It's not surprising then that Jesus said this centurion had great faith. This high degree of faith was the result of his great understanding.

The faith of the woman with the issue of blood came only after she had heard of Jesus. Again, the order is first hearing, then believing. Faith comes as a result of what we hear. In fact, Jesus even said, *"Take heed what you hear: with what measure you mete, it shall be measured to you: and unto you that hear shall more be given"* (Mark 4:24). In other words, it's important not only *what* we hear, but *how* we hear it. This is talking about an understanding. Hearing it in the ear should lead to an understanding in the heart.

Summary

It's commendable to pray. It's necessary and needful. It's a wise man who will pray, and pray consistently. The mistake that some people have made is to use their prayer life to try to get faith. But we don't pray to get faith, we pray **because** of our faith. To get faith we go to the Word of God, for *"faith cometh by hearing and hearing by the word of God."* With that faith we then pray to release that faith.

For example, to get saved we don't pray and ask God to give us faith for salvation. Instead, we go to God's Word and read that God is not willing that any should perish. Then we read that whosoever shall call upon the name of the Lord shall be saved. *From these scriptures we get faith* that God will save us if we pray. We understand the will of God from the Word of God.

Most Christians understand this for salvation, yet when it comes to receiving healing, the promises of God, etc., they throw away what they already understand about faith and blindly start praying for faith. Actually, it's a waste of time, breath, and energy to pray for faith. As in salvation, we go to the Word of God to find the scriptures that cover our particular need. From those scriptures we get the necessary faith to receive that which we need in prayer.

We also see from the centurion in Matthew chapter 8 that great faith is the result of a great understanding. From Jesus in Matthew chapter 16 we see that little faith is the result of a little understanding. The answer then in obtaining great faith comes from living in the Word of God. We read it, think it, contemplate it, meditate it, listen to it, and study it. Understanding it in our heart comes from dissecting it and then putting in together again over and over in our thinking. We live it, breathe it, walk it, and talk it.

Faith comes by hearing, and hearing by the Word of God. Once we hear it, if we'll meditate on it, we can expect the Holy Spirit to make it become real to us. Jesus said that the Holy Spirit would lead and guide us into all truth (John 16:13). Therefore, it's up to us to allow us to be led and guided. As we begin to comprehend the truth of God's Word, it's then up to us to start implementing it. Faith makes its greatest strides as we incorporate it in daily living. Like a muscle, faith develops and grows as it's exercised.

CHAPTER
15

HOW FAITH GROWS

We are bound to thank God always for you brethren, as it is meet, because your FAITH GROWETH EXCEEDINGLY...

- 2 Thessalonians 1:3

We understand from Paul's letter to the church in Thessalonica that faith grows. In the Bible there are numerous references to different degrees of faith (as seen in chapter 12) — weak faith (Romans 4:19), strong faith (Romans 4:20), little faith (Matthew 14:31), and great faith (Matthew 8:10). The fact that Jesus upbraided the disciples on several occasions for their little faith shows us that *the disciples* had the final say on whether or not their faith was little or great. If the disciples didn't have the ability to determine their development of faith, Jesus would have been unjust to upbraid them.

From this then we see that *we* are the ones responsible in whether or not our faith grows. If our faith remains weak we

151

have no one to blame but us. We certainly can't blame God, because He's done His part by giving us the measure of faith when we got saved. Notice:

For I say, through the grace given unto me, *to every man that is among you (in the church)*, not to think of himself more highly than he ought to think; but to think soberly, ACCORDING AS GOD HATH DEALT TO EVERY MAN (IN THE BODY OF CHRIST) THE MEASURE OF FAITH.

- Romans 12:3

This measure of faith that we were given when we received Jesus Christ is the faith that, according to 1 John 5:4, will help us overcome the world. Notice also that Paul called it *your* faith — *"We are bound to thank God always for you brethren, as it is meet, because YOUR FAITH groweth exceedingly..."*. This measure of faith has been given to us, it belongs to us, it's *our* faith. Because it belongs to us it's our responsibility to see that it grows.

So how does faith grow? It's simple, it grows by using it. We learn to trust God by trusting God. We learn to believe God by believing God. We learn to use our faith by using our faith. It's like anything else, if we want to learn to play the piano we learn by playing the piano. If we want to learn to drive a car we learn by driving a car. If we want to learn to hit a baseball we learn by hitting baseballs.

Really, it should be no mystery as to how faith grows. Usually, people who are sick concentrate on using their faith for healing. People who are poor concentrate on using their faith for prosperity. Whatever the area is that we're lacking in our lives is usually the area that we concentrate on first in learning to use our faith. As we use it, our faith-muscle, so to speak, begins to develop.

This is why some people have erroneously thought that God sends problems on people to develop their faith. When they found themselves in a crisis they had no choice but to use their faith. As they came out of the difficulty that they were in, they found that their faith was strengthened, and wrongly assumed then that God must've put that problem on them so that their faith would grow.

No, God doesn't put problems on people to develop their faith. Certainly their faith grew because they were using their faith, but that's why it grew — not because they had a problem, but because they were using their faith. There are so many problems in the world that there's no need for God to have to send a problem your way. All you have to do is start using your faith on any one of the many problems already around you and you'll be able to exercise your faith.

If God sent problems to develop people's faith then it's a shame that God didn't realize that he hadn't sent enough problems to the disciples, for their faith was little, and it exasperated Jesus in having to deal continuously with their little faith. I mean, how could Jesus upbraid the disciples for their little faith if it was up to God to make sure that problems came their way so that they could have great faith? Shouldn't Jesus have been upset with God for not giving the disciples enough problems so that they wouldn't have little faith?

Surely the reader can see the absurdity of such reasoning. The reason that Jesus upbraided the disciples for their little faith was *because it was the disciple's fault for their little faith*. Evidently then, it's not up to God to send problems our way to develop our faith. So if problems are coming our way, it's not because God is sending them our way to develop our faith.

God doesn't send problems. Problems are coming our way because there's a devil in the world and he's sending them to try to destroy us, not to build us up. If only people would realize this. Cancer doesn't come to people to make them more spiritual. Cancer comes to people to kill them. The devil is a hideous taskmaster and he sends all of the hell that he can to steal, kill, and destroy (John 10:10). The purpose of problems is not for building people up but for tearing them down. But if we'll learn to use our faith we can overcome any sickness, any disease, any financial difficulty, and any problem that would come our way.

The development of faith, as noted in chapter 12, can be compared to the development of a weightlifter's muscles. When a person first begins to lift weights, a trainer will start them with a light weight easily within their ability to repeatedly lift. As they become comfortable with that weight, a trainer will then add between 2 and 5 pounds to push their muscles a little further. Once the added weight is comfortable another 2 to 5 pounds will be added. Over time another 2 to 5 pounds will be added, and then eventually another 2 to 5 pounds. As this process is repeated again and again by periodically adding 2 to 5 pounds the weightlifter will be able to exercise with 200 pounds just as easy, if not easier than he was with 100 pounds a year earlier. We develop our muscles by using them. Likewise, we develop our faith by using it. The apostle James bears this out:

Seest thou how (Abraham's) faith wrought with his works, and by (his) works was faith made perfect?
- James 2:22

The words "perfect" and "works" leave a connotation that's not exactly accurate. A better rendering for "works" would be *"actions,"* and the better rendering for "perfect" would be *"mature, or complete."* Any good reference Bible will point this out. As such James 2:22 would read like this:

Seest thou how his faith wrought with his actions, and BY HIS ACTIONS WAS HIS FAITH MADE MATURE?

In other words, Abraham's faith matured by using it. As we use our faith it grows and develops. This is why it's not wise for someone to wait until they've been diagnosed with cancer before they decide to learn to develop their faith. If beginning weightlifters would try to lift 400 pounds when they've never lifted more than 100 pounds they wouldn't be able to lift it, regardless of how sincere they may be about trying to lift 400 pounds. It's beyond the ability of their muscles. But if they'll start small and develop into it their muscles will easily be able to handle 400 pounds and even more.

It's so important to start developing our faith as soon as we hear about it. It doesn't make sense to wait until a life-or-death crisis comes before we decide to try to develop our faith. That would be akin to a contractor waiting until a thunderstorm blows in before he tries to pour a concrete foundation to build a house. Instead, a contractor waits for a nice sunny day to lay a concrete foundation for building a house. If the foundation gets laid while the weather is pleasant, he can build the rest of the house in the rain if he has to. Likewise, if we'll lay a foundation for faith while life is somewhat pleasant, so to speak, we can get the rest of our faith developed even if we have to develop it in a storm.

It certainly makes sense to start developing our faith on small problems while life is relatively smooth. Start believing God for extra money to buy a new pair of shoes, or a new suit, or a new dress. Use your faith for the healing of a cold, or a headache, or a backache, or a rash. What's most important is that we get started believing God for something. It brings pleasure to God when He sees His children making the effort to grow spiritually and to develop their faith. It's necessary for us to start exercising this measure of faith. As we use it we're putting pressure on our faith like a weight puts pressure on a muscle. As it expands and contracts it gets stronger.

An excellent illustration of this is found in the story of David and Goliath. As David was explaining to Saul why he knew that he could defeat Goliath he recalled how he had previously beaten and killed both a lion and a bear:

And David said moreover, THE LORD THAT DELIVERED ME OUT OF THE PAW OF THE LION, AND OUT OF THE PAW OF THE BEAR, HE WILL DELIVER ME OUT OF THE HAND OF THIS

PHILISTINE.

- 1 Samuel 17:37

David was aware that he hadn't beaten these wild beasts because of his own strength. He recognized that he slew them because God had helped him. As a result of his realizing that the Lord had delivered him out of their paws he was convinced that God would help him do the same against a similar, yet more serious threat. Some people would call this presumptuous, but the Bible calls this strong faith.

The point is, though, that because of David's successful faith exploits, his faith had grown to such a point that he was ready to tackle an even more serious difficulty. David was ready to take on Goliath because he had proven his faith in smaller problems. The lesson is, before we face the Goliath's of life let's exercise our faith on the lions and bears of life. If the lions and bears of life seem too formidable then start with the mice, cats, and dogs of life. It's important to at least get started with something. Using our faith against colds, aches, and fevers, or for shoes, ties, and gloves is a good place to get started.

158

CHAPTER 16

FIND THE SCRIPTURE THAT COVERS YOUR NEED OR DESIRE (AND FORGIVE)

> **So then faith cometh by hearing, and hearing by the word of God.**
>
> **- Romans 10:17**

Since faith comes by hearing the Word of God, obviously then, our need or desire would have to be found in the Word of God in order for us to have faith to receive it. Therefore, to receive something *by faith*, that "thing" would have to be promised in the Word of God. If we get outside of God's Word, that is, if we can't find a verse with a promise, then we don't have a faith-leg, so to speak, to stand on.

The only assurance we have that God will answer our prayer is to ask for something that Jesus purchased for us at Calvary or for that which God has promised. If we have the promise on paper we can have faith to receive it. If we don't have the promise on paper we can't have faith to receive it.

As the apostle Paul said in Romans 1:16:

**For I am not ashamed of the _gospel of Christ_ (i.e.
the _Word of God_): for _it_ is the power of God unto...**

Notice it says that God's Word is the power of God _unto_.
Or it could be said this way — _God's power is released in
conjunction with God's Word_. Wherever God's Word is,
God's power is inherently there. When that promise is acted
upon in faith, the power of God will manifest itself to fulfill
that "Word" in that person's life. Simply put, _God's Word is
the foundation upon which receiving the promises of God is
built upon_.

It's always exciting when someone who asks for prayer
about a certain need, say healing for example, comes by
saying, *"1 Peter 2:24 and Matthew 8:17 tell me that healing
belongs to me. Since the Word of God tells me that it's mine,
I want you to agree with me. I believe I'll receive it now."*

Or, *"1 Timothy 1:7 says that God hasn't given me a spirit
of fear. Since God's Word tells me that I shouldn't be fearful,
I believe I'll now sleep at night peacefully without fear of
worry, or even nightmares."*

You see, these people's faith has a foundation built upon
the Word of God. They've found the necessary scriptures that
cover their particular need. So they have a godly assurance
that they can ask for it. They can expect their prayer to be
answered because they have the necessary Bible chapter and
verse.

Here's another example — *"The doctor says it's impossible for me to have children. But I just read in Psalm 127:3 that children are a heritage of the Lord. Since the word 'heritage' means something that comes or belongs to a person by reason of birth, this verse means that I can have children, because I'm a part of the family of God. Therefore, I believe I'll receive my healing now."*

Another example — *"I'm flying to Indianapolis, and I read in Psalm 91:11 that God has given his angels charge over me to protect me wherever I go. So I'm going to trust God, and I'm going to enjoy the flight. I will get there safely by plane."*

Again, these people have a reason for faith because they have the scriptures that cover their particular needs. They can have a solid and definite exercise of faith because they have a solid and definite foundation. Jeremiah 1:12 states, *"...for I (God) will hasten my word to perform it."* The word "hasten" in this verse more literally means, *"to watch over."* In other words, God is telling us that He watches over **His** Word to perform it. God is searching throughout the ends of the earth for people who will act in faith on **His** Word. God has gladly promised to do anything *found in His Word* for anyone who will believe it and receive it.

As we saw in Romans 1:16, the power of God works in conjunction with the Word of God. So if the Word of God isn't present, the power doesn't have anything to work with. So if the power of God isn't working in a particular area of our lives, then evidently the Word of God is not active in that particular area of our lives. *We must have the scripture cover-*

ing our particular need or desire if we are to expect God to move in that particular area. No word no power. No power no Word. The two work hand-in-hand.

The Importance Of Forgiveness

Therefore I say unto you, What things soever ye desire, when ye pray, believe that ye receive them, and ye shall have them. AND WHEN YE STAND PRAYING, FORGIVE, if ye have aught against any: that your Father also which is in heaven may forgive you your trespasses. But if ye do not forgive, neither will your Father which is in heaven forgive your trespasses.
- Mark 11:24-26

Jesus told an interesting story found in Matthew chapter 18 about a man who was forgiven a great financial debt by a certain king. When a reckoning was to be made the king commanded that this man, his wife, and children be sold as slaves to offset the tremendous debt that this man owed him. This man then fell to the ground and begged for patience. He promised the king that he would pay him back everything. For whatever reason, the king then had compassion on him, and instead of just giving him time to pay back the debt, which in itself would have been wonderful, the king forgave the entire debt and allowed him and his family to go free!

But this is where the story takes an unusual turn. It so happened that this man who was forgiven the great debt had a fellow servant who owed him a very small debt, a hundred pence. Sometime after he had left the king's presence he went out to his fellow servant, grabbed him by the throat, and had him thrown into prison until he was paid back his money.

When the king heard what had been done he was wroth. He said, *"O thou wicked servant, I forgave thee all that debt, because thou desiredst me: Shouldest not thou also have had compassion on thy fellow servant, even as I had pity on thee?"* The king then had this man thrown into prison.

So what does this have to do with faith? Read Jesus' concluding remarks in this story:

Shouldest not thou also have had compassion on thy fellow servant, even as I had pity on thee? And his lord was wroth, _and delivered him to the tormentors_, till he should pay all that was due unto him. _So likewise_ shall my heavenly Father do also unto you, _if ye from your hearts forgive not_ every one his brother their trespasses.
- Matthew 18:33-35

We have no right to expect God to answer our prayers if we refuse to forgive the trespasses of others. The tormentor (the devil and demons) will have free reign to work destruction in our lives. Sickness, disease, financial woes, family problems, etc. will have easy access in our lives. _Regardless of how much faith we are exercising, unforgiveness will stop the power of God from flowing into our lives_.

Forgiveness Is Mandatory

Unforgiveness has a direct bearing on whether or not our faith is able to work. We can pull all the right levers and push all the correct buttons but nothing will happen. We can make all the right confessions and act on the Word of God appropriately, but faith will be stymied.

"Yes, but you don't know what they did to me!"

No, most likely I don't. Whether or not I know what they did to you has absolutely nothing to do with the workings of your faith. Even if I fully understood your feelings and had an understanding as to why you're upset with that person, it still won't change the fact that you'll be in the power of the tormentor.

Is it that important that I have a full understanding of your problems and why you're mad at the world? You might gain my sympathy and I might feel sorry for you, but again, that won't change your circumstances. *What is more important to you, having your feelings understood, or breaking the power of the tormentor in your life?* The obvious answer is that it should be more important for the power of the enemy to be broken in your life.

Of course, people are going to do wrong to you sometime somewhere. Most people don't play fair. They're only concerned about what's in it for them. If you happen to have what they want, they'll use you to obtain their goal. Once they've got it, they're ready to forget you and go to the next person. *Don't make the mistake of letting their dumb action back you into a corner of unforgiveness*.

I'D RATHER FORGIVE AND BE HEALED THAN TO BE JUSTIFIABLY MAD AT SOMEONE AND STAY SICK.

Regardless of how you've been mistreated, or what others have derogatorily said about you, or how you've been taken advantage of, by our refusing to forgive we're shutting off the tap to God's blessings. From reading Mark 11:24-25 the greatest hindrance to the power of faith is the refusal to forgive.

God Sees Everything

The common tendency of many is to assume that because we have to forgive, then the other person is somehow getting off scott-free. Of course, nothing could be further from the truth. We will all one day stand before the judgement seat of Christ to give an account for all that was done while in the flesh, both good and bad (2 Corinthians 5:10). Those who have purposely wronged you will one day have to give an answer for the action that they took against you. God, who knows all and sees all (Hebrews 4:13), will one day openly deal with each situation.

Too many times I've seen ministers, who were hurt by someone in their congregation, remain bitter and unforgiving toward that person or persons. Then, I've seen many congregational members, who were hurt by something their pastor said or did, become bitter and unforgiving toward him. I've seen evangelists become bitter over something a pastor did to them in one of their meetings. I've seen family members hurt and bitter toward other family members, and friends bitter toward past friends, parents of children bitter toward parents of other children, and people bitter toward other people they've never even met.

It's our job to leave our hurts with God. It's imperative that we turn each situation over to God. When we carry a grudge and become bitter, the *only* person that we're hurting is us. *When we refuse to forgive we're not hurting the other person who wronged us.* We might make that person mad by giving them the cold shoulder, but in the final analysis, when all is said and done, our unforgiveness hurts and literally destroys us.

How, you may ask? *Unforgiveness stops our faith from working and leaves us in the hands of the tormentor.* Regardless of how bad the situation may seem, compared to the debt of sin that's been forgiven us, their wrong can hardly even be seen with a microscope. If God has chosen to forgive us our incredulous, monstrous-type debt of sin, God expects us to forgive the nickel and dime type debts with each other.

Faith Works By Love

For in Jesus Christ neither circumcision availeth any thing, nor uncircumcision; BUT FAITH WHICH WORKETH BY LOVE.
- Galations 5:6

Faith works by love. Without love faith *cannot* work. Without forgiveness flowing from our heart, faith can't produce. The only way that our faith will produce anything in our lives is by having a forgiving heart. Don't let the devil trip your faith by reminding you of people who have hurt you. Yes, they may have wronged you, but life is too exciting and God has too much to offer for you to get tripped driving down a dead-end road. Forgive and enjoy abundant provision.

CHAPTER
17

FAITH HAS ACTION

Even so faith, if it hath not works (action) is dead, being alone.

- James 2:17

Simply put, actions of faith are those things that we do because we believe that God has answered our prayer. These actions are not based on what we can see but upon that which we can't see. For example, if we've prayed for a certain financial need to be met, say $10,000, faith now says that the need is met. Yet our checkbook says that we're still behind the needed $10,000. If we choose to walk by faith our actions will have to correspond to that which we say we believe.

In other words, even though we don't have the $10,000 in our possession we're now going to stop worrying *as if* we actually had the $10,000. We're going to act foot-loose and fancy-free, so to speak, because of what we believe. We're living now by what we believe, not by what we see. If we would live by what we see we'd worry and fret and be tempted to pull our hair out. To the nominal Christian watching us who doesn't understand faith it appears there's a fine line between us being crazy and acting on the Word of God. To them it appears that we're denying certain financial facts and living in a pseudo make-believe world, as if the pressure just got to be too much for us mentally and we've pulled out of the real world to live in our own world of make-believe.

Nothing could be farther from the truth. We're not denying reality, we're choosing to have faith in God for the changing of reality. Yes, we recognize that we're short the $10,000, but our faith says that God answered our prayer and we *believe* that we have the $10,000, with the assurance that we'll physically and materially have the $10,000 before it's due. We're choosing not to worry because we believe it's now taken care of. If we continue to worry after we pray, in effect, we're saying that we don't believe we'll have the money in time. In other words, our actions are saying that we don't believe God has answered our prayer. If we persist in worrying, our actions will negate that which we say we believe, and our faith won't produce the needed $10,000.

Using healing as another example, suppose someone has asked God to heal them of cancer. By faith they now say they're healed of cancer. The medical report, however, says that they're still dying of cancer. For them to walk by faith it means that their actions will now have to correspond with that which they say they believe. They're going to have to stop worrying about dying, because if they continue to worry about dying their actions are saying that they don't believe that God has answered their prayer. It will hinder their faith.

Faith Has Action

How would you act if you hadn't been diagnosed with cancer? Most likely you'd be making plans for your day-to-day schedule, plans for travel, plans for certain things at church, or whatever. So if you believe that God has answered your prayer for healing, you wouldn't be worrying about dying and you'd be going about your plans for daily life as usual. *(For questions about taking medicine, see chapter 12.)*

3 Ways To Act Out Your Faith

1. Don't Worry

There are 3 primary ways for our actions to correspond with our faith, one of which is by refusing to worry. Simply put, worry and anxiety is the fear that something bad is going to happen or may happen. It's an action that says we don't have any idea what's going to happen, but if something does happen it's probably going to be bad. People who worry live in a constant state of apprehension and mental uneasiness until they know that everything is going to work out alright. So if a person prays and asks God to work out a particular situation, if they continue to worry they're not believing that God is working everything out.

Always remember that faith has to do with that which can't be seen. If we can see that everything is going to work out alright there's no need to have to believe. When things look bad and we've prayed, we have to act *as if* we can see that everything is going to work out alright. The truth is, we can't *see* how it will work out but we *believe* it will work out. And because we believe it, we're acting like we would if we could see it. We're refusing to worry.

Some people think that they can worry while they're believing. This is impossible. We can only do one or the other. Certainly the temptation to worry will come to our minds while we're believing. After all, we're *believing*, not *seeing*. Because we can't see it, the pressure to worry will definitely come to our minds. Those of us who choose to walk by faith have to cast down these imaginations in our thinking. Jesus said it this way:

> **...be not afraid, _only_ believe.**
> **- Mark 5:36**

> **...fear not, believe _only_.**
> **- Luke 8:50**

The word "only" in these verses is significant. It means, *"this and no other."* In other words, Jesus is confirming the fact that we can't worry and believe at the same time. If we are to believe _only_ it means that there's not any other ingredient that can be added into the mix, certainly not fear. To believe, we have to refuse to fear, reason being that fear is in the opposite direction of faith. If we *believe* that God has answered our prayer, it means that we're expecting something *good* to happen. If we're *worrying,* it means that we're expecting something *bad* to happen. So how can we expect something good to happen while we're expecting something bad to happen? *It can't be done.* Worry is the opposite of faith. People who believe must act like they believe.

2. Praise And Thanksgiving

Faith acts while the answer can't be seen *in the same manner* that sight acts when the answer can be seen. How

170

would we act if we prayed for $10,000 and then one day later actually had the $10,000 in our hands? We would automatically thank God for His provision and praise His name. How would we act if we prayed for the healing of cancer and if, in the following CAT scan and blood test, there was not any trace of the cancer? We would automatically thank God for our healing and praise His name.

Therefore faith will praise and thank God in this same manner for the $10,000 and the healing of cancer *before* either of them can be seen. We praise God because we *believe* that our prayer is answered. No, we don't see the money and no, we don't feel the healing, but we're just as convinced of it as if we already could see and feel it. Therefore we're praising and thanking God *by faith.*

Faith glorifies God because it *believes* the answer to be so. Sight glorifies God because it *sees* the answer to be so. Yet before we'll ever be able to see it we first have to believe it. If we believe it we'll praise and thank God for it by faith. We're just so happy and full of joy because we believe we have our answer. Yes, we're excited and looking forward to being able to see it and to feel it. I mean, that's why we prayed in the first place. We're praising and thanking God because we're convinced of that which can't yet be seen. That is, we're fully persuaded *in our heart* that God has given it to us and will bring it to pass. Take notice of *when* Abraham was giving glory to God:

He (Abraham) staggered not at the promise of God through unbelief; but was strong in faith, GIVING GLORY TO GOD; and being fully persuaded that, what

171

he had promised, he was able also to perform.
- Romans 4:20-21

Abraham was giving glory to God *before* God had performed the miracle. It's easy to give glory to God after the miracle can be seen. Anyone can do that, but not everyone can give glory to God *before* the miracle can be seen. It requires faith to praise and thank God when the situation hasn't appeared to have changed, while your body is still hurting and your creditors are still calling.

If we could travel into the past in a time machine to the days of Joshua, a person of faith would rejoice and thank God while the walls of Jericho were still standing. He would praise God before the walls had fallen. Yes, the walls are still up. Yes, the inhabitants still possess the city. But he's rejoicing because, regardless of what it looks like, God has told him that the city belongs to him. Since it belongs to him he has the assurance the walls are going to fall. So he's praising God for what he now believes is his, in spite of the walls.

The person who believes that God has answered his prayer thanks God, not because he sees any change, but because he believes it's already been taken care of. His actions of faith are those of praise. He praises God for his answer while it's in its *invisible* form. He recognizes the fact that his answer will be visible, but praises God by faith for that which is still invisible.

3. Speak Right Words

The person who believes that God has answered his prayer

will talk differently than the person who doesn't believe that God has answered his prayer. He who doesn't believe will use his words to ask for prayer again. He who believes will use his words to speak words of faith. Instead of saying things like, *"I wish I could get healed,"* he'll say, *"I believe I am healed."* You can always locate a person's faith by what they say.

The initial way we act our faith is to change what we're saying. There's no need to ask for prayer again and again. I mean, why should we ask for prayer again if we believe that God answered our first prayer? Someone says, *"But I don't feel any better yet."* Of course you don't feel better yet, you have to <u>*believe*</u> that you're healed first.

This is so important. Mark 11:24 does not say, *"when you pray <u>feel</u> that you receive them."* It says, *"when you pray, <u>believe</u> that you receive them."* The order is undeniable — *"believe that ye receive them, and ye shall have them."* In other words, we first have to believe that we have it before we can feel that we have it.

I realize that you want to feel better. We all want to feel better. But we'll never feel better until we first believe that we're healed. So just because we don't feel better it doesn't mean that we should pray again. It means that we need to start believing. Faith will produce all of the feelings we'll ever need or want. Just saying another prayer again without believing is repeating the same mistake of the first prayer. Three hours later you'll pray for healing again. Three hours after that you'll pray for healing again. Tomorrow afternoon you'll pray for healing again. The need here is not another prayer, the need is to believe. In the midst of the pain and discomfort we act our faith by saying, *"I believe that I'm healed. I believe that God answered my prayer."*

What About Physical Actions?

Some have asked, *"If I'm in a wheelchair should I try to stand?"*

The fact that you had to ask, *"Should I TRY to stand?"*, shows that you should stay seated for the time being. Faith doesn't have anything to do with *trying*. When you truly believe that you're healed there will be something on the inside of you that will lead you to stand. Trying it won't even be in your thinking, you'll automatically start doing it.

Sadly, I've seen sincere people attempting to do different kinds of physical actions hoping it would cause God to move on their behalf. Some people have poured their medicine down the drain, while others have stumbled out of wheelchairs, while others will literally almost swing from a chandelier, thinking that what they're doing is what's needed to get God to move. They call it faith, but just because you call a cat a dog doesn't make it a dog. And just because they call it faith doesn't mean it is faith.

Every once in awhile I'll read in the newspaper about some family who won't give their child some medicine, such as insulin, or they won't seek medical help for their sickly child, all under the guise of what they call faith. They think that by asking for a doctor's help it will hinder God from healing them, or by not asking for a doctor's help it will force God to intervene in their situation. Invariably, the sick person or child will die, sometimes with extreme suffering in the latter stages. I'm always saddened by these stories and feel sorry for these misguided people. I wouldn't question their sincerity for one second, but sincerity and faith are two different things.

Certain physical actions of faith will come as a result of an overflow of what's in the heart. For a lack of a better word, they're second nature, that is, they're actions that are not premeditated. They're what happens on the spur of the moment. They're what we do without having to take 10 minutes trying to talk us in to doing. We do certain things automatically because it just seems to be the right thing to do. If we're in bed we just get up. If we're in a wheelchair we just stand. If we have to spend a few minutes thinking about what we should do, we probably shouldn't do anything.

Think back to Peter in Matthew chapter 14 when he got out of the boat. The disciples were in a small boat out in the sea during a tumultuous storm. When Jesus, who was walking on water, bid Peter to join him out on the water by saying, *"Come,"* Peter, *without even thinking*, immediately climbed out of the boat and started walking on the water. While all of his mental and spiritual energies were concentrated on Jesus and what He said, Peter was successful in walking on the water. When Peter started *thinking* about what he was doing, that is when he took notice of the waves, rain, and wind, and began to sink.

When we start thinking about what we're doing, it's time to get back into the boat. We're concentrating more on *our* actions than we are on what God's Word has said. Physical actions should be those things that are almost involuntary. It's like when a doctor taps our kneecap with a rubber mallet. Our leg just automatically responds with a kick. When we believe that God has answered our prayer, if there are any physical actions to be taken, they'll be those things that we do without having to mentally plan them.

We also learn from the son who *began to amend* in John chapter 4 that there may only be certain limited physical actions you could take anyway. In other words, if you're only *beginning to amend* you certainly wouldn't be able to do what you could do if you were *fully* amended. The key, then, is to do that which you're able. Certainly the person who is paralyzed wants to get up, but until the power of God is manifest in his body, he may not be able to get up. So if you're still committed to the thinking that you've got to do something physically, start first by just moving your toes.

Say What You Believe

Don't worry about what you should physically be doing. Concentrate on what you're believing and saying. The primary way that we act our faith is to *say* what we believe. Think about the greatest miracle of all, the new birth of the human spirit. You didn't stop smoking and drinking to get saved, you stopped smoking and drinking because you already were saved. You stopped doing these things because there was an overflow of salvation coming from your heart. Your initial response to the gospel message was to first believe it and then say it. The actions just took care of themselves.

Likewise, our initial response to any part of the gospel,

whether it's healing, prosperity, the promises of God, etc., is to first believe it and then say it. When we believe it our first response should be to say it. What Paul said in 2 Corinthians 4:17 is as definitive as any scripture along this line:

We having the same spirit of faith, according as it is written, I believed, AND THEREFORE HAVE I SPOKEN; we also believe, AND THEREFORE SPEAK.

Take note of the word "therefore." It means, *"because of this."* As such 2 Corinthians 4:13 would read this way:

We having the same spirit of faith, according as it written, AND BECAUSE OF THIS, I HAVE SPOKEN; we also believe, AND BECAUSE OF THIS, SPEAK.

In other words, because we believe, our first response should be to speak. Our primary action of faith is to _say with our mouth_ what we believe in our heart. If we've prayed for salvation we should _say_ that we believe we're saved. If we've prayed for healing we should _say_ that we believe we're healed. If we've prayed for money we should _say_ that we believe our need is met. Even though we may not see or feel anything yet, our believing motivates us to act in a corresponding way by saying it with our mouth.

CHAPTER 18

WE SET THE TIME

(WE'RE NOT WAITING ON GOD, GOD IS WAITING ON US.)

...if I may but touch his clothes, I shall be whole.
- woman with the issue of blood, Mark 5:28

This woman had an issue of blood for 12 years. Her condition was so severe that her body couldn't repair itself, for she had undergone many different treatments from numerous doctors, yet she never got any better. Actually, she consistently kept getting worse. In addition, every last dollar that she possessed had been spent on medical expenses. She was broke and dying.

This is where the story changes. From someone, or most likely, from many people, she had heard of the healings of a prophet from Galilee named Jesus. When she did she determined to be healed. She said, *"If I may but touch his clothes, I shall be whole."* Actually, the Greek text says, *"For she **kept** saying, If I may but touch his clothes, I shall be whole."*

In other words, this woman was continually saying over and over, *"If I can touch his clothes I'll be healed. If I can touch his clothes I'll be healed. If I can touch his clothes I'll be healed."* When she arrived at an area where Jesus had been ministering but had already left, she obtained directions to where Jesus was next headed. She said, *"I'm going to find him and when I do, if I can touch his clothes I'm going to be healed."*

Finally, she saw the multitudes surrounding Jesus and she determinedly worked her way through the crowd. She kept saying, *"If I can touch his clothes I shall be whole."*

Then there he was.

"I'm going to touch his clothes now and be healed." She reached her hand out and touched the hem of his garment. When she did, God responded to her faith. Verse 30 states that the healing virtue of God flowed out of Jesus into her body and healed her body of that plague.

When Jesus realized that healing power had gone out of his body he knew that someone had touched him *in faith*. He immediately stopped and asked, *"Who touched my clothes?"* The disciples responded, *"What do you mean, 'Who touched you?' Everyone here is trying to touch you."* Then the woman immediately came forward and told Jesus in front of the crowd all that she had done. Jesus concluded by saying,

Daughter, thy faith hath made thee whole; go in peace, and be whole of thy plague."

The Woman Set The Time For Her Healing

In this account we see that, up to this point, Jesus hadn't known anything about this woman. He hadn't used his faith with her like he had with others by commanding her body to be healed. He didn't even know who it was that had touched him. He hadn't laid his hands on her, hadn't spoken a word of healing to her body, and hadn't ministered to her in any way.

Instead, *this woman set the time for her healing*. It was *her faith* that had determined when she would receive. *She* was the one who made the appointment with God for her healing. It was *the woman* who determined that she would be healed when *she* touched his clothes. *Instead of Jesus reprimanding her for doing this, He commended her for doing this!*

Plainly, God is ready and waiting to answer our prayers. *His* time is *our* time. To receive something from God, it's *never* a matter of us twisting His arm. It's a matter of us finally taking God at His Word. God is waiting on *us*.

When this woman with the issue of blood said, *"I'll be healed when I touch his clothes,"* God was thrilled! When the centurion in Matthew 8:8 said to Jesus, *"The moment you speak the word my servant will be healed,"* God was thrilled! God is more desirous to answer our prayers than we are desirous to receive them.

It's to our benefit to set the time to believe that we receive. I've heard people say such things as, *"Whenever God is good and ready He'll heal me,"* or, *"I'll be healed sometime."* The problem with this is that it always leaves the answer out in some unknown, indefinite future. God is good and ready _now_. God isn't waiting to heal you "sometime." _He's waiting to heal you when you set the time to believe_.

"Sometime" Is Not Definite

It's sad, but have you ever noticed that the people who are always waiting on God to heal them "sometime" never get healed? The reason is because faith is not "sometime," faith is "now." Hebrews 11:1 states, *"...Now faith is...".*

In order for faith to work there must be a *definite* time that _we_ plan to *"believe that we receive it."* Even though the whole multitude was touching Jesus (Mark 5:31), they didn't receive anything because, unlike this woman with the issue of blood, their faith hadn't set the time for their healing. They only touched Jesus out of curiosity, _wondering_ if anything would happen. Or possibly out of desperation, not faith.

Notice the "set" time the following people expected to receive their answer:

...come and lay thy hands on her, that she may be healed, and she shall live.
- Jairus, Mark 5:23

...speak the word only, and my servant shall be healed.
- centurion, Matthew 8:8

182

...If I may touch but his clothes, I shall be whole.
- woman with an issue of blood, Mark 5:28

...that they might only touch the hem of his garment: and as many as touched were made perfectly whole.
- many people in the crowds, Matthew 14:36

It's interesting to note that after this woman with the issue of blood was healed by touching Jesus' garment, others determined later to do the same. You'll remember that this woman had told Jesus in front of the whole multitude what she had done:

"And when the woman saw that she was not hid, she came trembling, and falling down before him, she declared unto him BEFORE ALL THE PEOPLE for what cause she had touched him, and how she was healed immediately.

- Luke 8:47

When others had heard how this woman had received her healing, many stopped touching out of curiosity and started touching Jesus' clothes *in faith*. It's important to notice that God responded to the times that *they* set. These "set" times *were not initiated by God*, these "set" times *were initiated by the people*. It must be said again, God responded to the times that *they* set. Why? Because God is always ready and waiting to answer.

To receive one of the promises of God it is never a matter of us having to wait on God. Jesus said, *"What things soever ye desire, when* **YE** *pray, believe that ye receive them, and ye shall have them."* Jesus did **not** say, *"What things so ever ye desire, when God is good and ready, ye shall have them."*

The Responsibility Is *Ours* To Set The Time

Jesus gave **us** the *privilege* and the *responsibility* to set the time that we believe we receive. Whenever <u>we</u> choose to use our faith is the time that God responds. It is *our* responsibility to set a specific and definite time to believe that we receive.

Some have argued, *"God is sovereign. He doesn't have to respond to anything or any time that we set. He does what he wants to when he wants to. You can't order God around."*

The person who makes this statement has a mistaken understanding of the scriptures and the heart of God. First of all, Mark 11:24, among the many numerous scriptures, *has absolutely nothing to do with ordering God around*. Was the woman with the issue of blood ordering God around? Was the centurion in Matthew chapter 8 ordering God around? Of course not! The heart of God was, and is, extremely desirous to reach out to help people.

Secondly, Mark 11:24 was not concocted by some selfish religious quack trying to satisfy his ego and religious instincts. Mark 11:24 was freely given to us *by Jesus*, which in turn, came from a loving, heavenly Father. Jesus plainly said on several occasions, *"...as my Father hath taught me, I speak these things"* (John 8:28). What Jesus said in Mark 11:24 was given to us *by God, our heavenly Father*, not by man. (See also John 14:13-14, John 15:7, John 16:23-24,

Matthew 18:19, Matthew 21:21-22, Matthew 17:20, Mark 9:23, etc.)

Thirdly, when we are setting a time to receive, we're not controlling God, _we're controlling us_! For example, if a friend called me on the phone and said, *"I want to meet with you to have dinner and fellowship."* So I said, *"That sounds good to me."* And they asked, *"When would be a good time to get together?"* And I said, *"Oh, anytime."* And they asked, *"Where would you like to meet?"* and I replied, *"Oh, anywhere."* If that is what is said, the chances of us getting together would be very slim. _We_ need to set a time and place. _I'm not controlling my friend, rather, I'm responding to his invitation_.

Likewise, when we are setting a time to receive from God, we are simply responding to God's open invitation to meet our needs. In so many words, God is saying, *"I'm ready when you're ready. Call on me and I will answer thee"* (Jeremiah 33:3, Isaiah 58:9, Psalm 91:15).

When we set the time to call upon God because of His wonderful invitation, God is ready to respond with the answer. When the woman with the issue of blood made the decision to receive her healing by touching the hem of Jesus' garment, God wasn't obeying an order given by a selfish, commanding egomaniac. Rather, God was responding with open arms to a person whose faith was reaching out in the only way she knew how. Her faith had pinpointed her time to receive.

The person who says, *"God will heal me sometime some-*

where, " is unknowingly keeping his healing out of reach. God is, like the man who offered me dinner, waiting for us to set a specific time to receive. *It's up to __us__ to set the time and the place.* God has given us many different ways to help us do this

Ways To Set The Time

1. Anointing With Oil.

According to James 5:14-15, we can call for the elders of the church to anoint us with oil in the name of the Lord. Obviously, the oil doesn't have any curative power in it. The power is in the prayer of faith (verse 15). The anointing with oil *sets the time* for us to receive.

God's purpose for this is to impact the spirit of the person being prayed for. We can feel the touch of the oil, and we can see the elders in the room praying for us. When this takes place something inside says, *"This is the moment that I'll be healed."* The time is set, the place is set, and the prayer of faith can do its job.

2. Laying On Of Hands

In Mark 16:18 Jesus said, *"...lay hands on the sick, and they shall recover."* This is another method that sets the time to receive healing. The key to the laying on of hands, like the anointing with oil, is the prayer of faith. When we feel the hands of the minister on our body it helps us to release our faith. It is helping us to set the time to receive. Our faith should be focused to the very moment that hands are laid upon us.

One common mistake that I've seen in some churches is to fall into a lackadaisical attitude about the laying on of hands, to let the familiarity become a routine, a form. Because some have seen church services where the laying on of hands is a common practice, the significance of what makes the laying on of hands so important and special becomes an empty ritual. They go through the motions, but they've left out the *purpose* for the motions — *to believe*. Believing, as with the anointing with oil, is what makes the laying on of hands work. We are to purposely believe that we receive when hands are laid upon us.

If you've found you in this situation of only going through the motions you can easily correct this. Simply make an inside adjustment in your spirit. Make the decision to purposely believe. Set the time, *ahead of time*, that you are going to believe that you receive your healing when hands are laid upon you. For example, *"At 8:45 p.m., when that minister lays his hands on me, I will be healed."* Then after prayer, say, *"At 8:45 p.m., when that preacher laid his hands upon me, I did receive my healing. I believe that I am now healed."*

3. Agreeing With Another Person

This method is found in Matthew 18:19. It says, *"...if two of you shall agree on earth as touching any thing that they shall ask, it shall be done for them of my Father which is in heaven."* When we agree in prayer with someone who is right there with us in the room, it is easy to remember exactly when, where, and what we prayed. We set the time to receive when our friend was with us in the room.

Again, it's the prayer of faith that moves the mountain, but the closeness of having a friend or loved one with us when we pray helps us to focus our faith to a specific time. We set the time by asking our "agree-er" to join with us in prayer.

4. When You Pray

The final method that I'm mentioning here is found in Mark 11:24. It says, *"What things so ever ye desire, **when YE pray**, believe that ye receive them, and ye shall have them." This is the method that's the most advantageous to us.* Our faith doesn't need to depend upon a minister's hands. It doesn't depend upon whether or not there is any anointing oil available. It doesn't depend upon the need to have another person with us. The only thing our faith needs is the written Word of God.

Regardless of where we are or who can be reached by phone, _we_ can pray the prayer of faith. We don't need to feel the anointing oil, or someone's hands, or to hear the voice of another's prayer. We simply pray our own prayers and believe that we receive them. *We believe that God hears and answers us simply because Jesus said that He would.*

Many, many times before I pray, I look at the calendar and clock. I make a mental note of the time and date, and then pray. Jesus told us in Mark 11:24 to set the time to believe that we receive *when we pray*. Therefore, I set the time to believe that I receive based upon when I pray.

CHAPTER 19

PUT THE ANSWER IN THE *PAST TENSE*

"...believe that ye receive them, and ye shall have them.

- Mark 11:24

Before the answer to our prayer comes to pass, we must first believe that God has already answered our prayer. Many people have the mistaken understanding that when the answer comes to pass is when God answers the prayer. But if we wait until the answer comes to pass before we believe that we have it, we never will have it. If we wait to see before we believe, we've reversed the law of faith. The law of faith is that we believe *before* we see. Seeing does not produce believing. Believing is what produces seeing.

One common mistake with some people is in not counting the work done. For example, some have said, *"I believe that*

God is killing the roots of my sickness day-by-day." The error in this, though, is in leaving part of the answer, if not most of the answer, *in the future*. In other words, they're saying that they weren't healed yesterday, and they're not healed today, but sometime in the upcoming weeks God will completely heal them. They're saying that God is progressively healing them by a continual, ongoing process.

This is incorrect. Certainly the manifestation of the healing could be a continual, ongoing process. *But our part, according to the Bible, is to reckon the healing completely done, once and for all. Faith says, "God has answered my prayer. He's not killing the roots of my sickness day-by-day. He's killed the sickness, period. I believe that I am healed."*

Sight Disagrees

Now "sight" may disagree with this statement. According to 2 Corinthians 5:7, we're not to walk by sight. We're to walk by faith. *Faith counts the work completely done.* The perfect example is Abraham. Romans 4:17 records what God said to Abraham in Genesis 17:5. Notice one part of this statement:

...I have made thee a *father*...

Obviously, to be a father you must have a child. Yet, when God said this Abraham did *not* have a child (and Sarah wasn't pregnant yet either). Nevertheless, God called Abraham a father *before* Isaac was conceived. Why? Because faith counts the work done.

The Work Must Be Counted Done

It's important to count the work done, once and for all. We don't say, *"I believe that God will heal me someday."* We don't say, *"I believe that God is healing me day-by-day."* We don't say, *"God has heard me and I'm waiting for him to heal me."* We <u>do</u> say, *"I believe that God has answered my prayer. God just healed me when I prayed. I believe that I am healed."* From this moment when we count the work done it will come to pass. Now it might come to pass hour-by-hour, or it might come to pass within 10 seconds. <u>*But how it comes to pass is something that we can't concern us with.*</u>

I've seen some people stop the healing process by getting back into the sight realm. Because they started feeling better, or because they started looking better, they unintentionally shifted from faith to sight. Instead of continuing to believe that they were healed because the Word of God said they were, they started believing that they were healed because they felt 20% better or because they looked 20% better.

When people do this, they're setting themselves up for a fall. If they start feeling bad again, the devil will put thoughts into their mind, such as, *"I guess I'm not healed after all."* At this point, it's easy to rely entirely on what we feel and see, and the healing can be lost.

If this happens, it's time to go back to square one. What was it that originally produced the 20% improvement in the feelings? Obviously it was the stand of faith. <u>*You believed*</u>

191

that you were healed because Jesus told you to believe it in Mark 11:24. Feelings had nothing to do with it when you prayed, therefore your feelings shouldn't have anything to do with it now if you're 20% better, 35% better, or even 95% better. Regardless of how the recovery transpires, we stay with what faith says until we're 100% well.

Faith counts the answer done. We say that our prayer was answered because God's Word says that it was answered, not because we can tell an improvement in our feelings. By sticking with what faith says there will be an improvement. Regardless of how it comes to pass, *our responsibility is to believe that we got it when we prayed by putting the answer in the past tense*.

TWO FINAL SUGGESTIONS

1. **Don't Put Unnecessary Pressure On You To Talk Your Faith In The Company Of Unbelievers.**

Some people think that if they pray for healing they have to tell everyone they come in contact with that they believe they're healed. Unfortunately, they think they're advancing the cause of faith, not realizing that they're probably hurting the cause of faith in the minds of those listening. This is all the more true with people who are just hearing about faith for the first time. They're sincere and, no doubt, mean well. But if this is new to them, most likely their faith isn't sufficiently developed. As such, if their prayer doesn't come to pass, the people who heard them tend to think that their _ex_-friend probably had a screw loose.

My advice is, wait until the answer to your prayer comes to pass. Once it does then you can tell all of your friends how you received it. It'll be a greater blessing to you and heavily influence their thinking. If they know that you had diabetes and injected yourself with insulin every day, and now know that you no longer have to, they'll be very interested in what happened with you.

Paul had an interesting comment along this line:

Hast thou faith? have it to thyself before God...
- Romans 14:22

In other words, don't let your faith be a stumbling block to others. If you'll bide your time your faith will make a tremendous impact for good on all the people you come in contact with.

When the Bible talks about confessing your faith it's not talking about a religious performance. The Pharisees in Jesus' day fell into this trap. When they prayed they stood on the street corners of their day and thought that they'd be heard for their much speaking. People who do such things are usually just misguided baby Christians, or, like the Pharisees, living in pride. According to Jesus, it's really just a waste of time and breath.

Really, just go to your prayer closet and tell God that you believe your prayer has been answered. Let Him know that you're standing on His Word. As your faith grows, and as your prayers come to pass,_people will start asking you what's going on in your life_. You'll have more than enough opportunities to be a witness for the things of God.

2. Meditate Constantly On The Word Of God

This book of the law shall not depart out of thy mouth; BUT THOU SHALT MEDITATE THEREIN DAY AND NIGHT, that thou mayest observe to do according to all that is written therein: for then thou shalt make thy way prosperous, and then thou shalt have good success.

- Joshua 1:8

The key to a victorious life of faith is to meditate constantly on the scriptures. Just because we read a book one time through or listen to a teaching tape one time through it doesn't mean that we have digested all that was taught. It's imperative to completely overhaul our minds, that is, if we want our life to be completely transformed for the good. Paul said it this way:

And be not conformed to this world: BUT BE YE TRANSFORMED BY THE RENEWING OF YOUR MIND, that ye may prove what is that good, and acceptable, and perfect, will of God.

- Romans 12:2

We are responsible for changing our thinking. As we grow, every person has been raised to think a certain way, some of it good, some of it bad. Our minds work very much like a computer. Whatever we put into it is what's going to come out of it. If we put math into it, math is going to come out of it. If we put science into it, science is going to come out of it. We can't expect social studies to come out of it if we haven't first put social studies into it.

Unfortunately, spiritually speaking, people want faith to come out of their spirit without their first having taken the time to load faith into it. They'll spend year after year after year loading doubt and unbelief into it, and then take two weeks to load a quick course on faith into it. Then they wonder why their faith won't produce. The problem is that they have a 4.0 gigabyte hard drive with 3.99 gigs of doubt and unbelief and only .01 gig of faith. The solution then, is to delete all the files of doubt and unbelief, and load in 4.0 gigs of faith.

Also, as much as the mind is like a computer, unfortunately, we can't delete memories, habits, and wrong teaching with the click of a mouse like we can a computer. We personally have to hand-carry each wrong teaching to the recycle bin and deal with it. And the way we clean our hard drive is by scriptural meditation. We have to replace old files with new files.

Based on how we were raised and scripturally taught, for some of us it may take more time to relearn. Quite frankly, it's easier to learn than it is to relearn. Relearning implies unlearning. We're going to have to unlearn some things before we can start to learn how to implement these spiritual laws and truths. As exciting as faith is, we're probably going to have to uproot a whole field full of trees of doubt and unbelief first.

How do we do this? By study and meditation on particular Bible truths. For example, since this book has been on faith I would recommend study and meditation on faith. After all, all that God offers is received by faith, and Hebrews 11:3 states that it's impossible to please God without faith. Therefore, faith is a vital part of the Christian walk.

I would recommend that you meditate constantly on Mark 11:24 day and night. Quote Mark 11:24 in your thinking over and over and over and over and over and over again and again and again and again and again. Take it apart in your mind and then put it back together. Then take it apart again and put it back together again. Then take it apart again and again, and put it back together again and again. Quote it over and over in your thinking 10,000 times until you comprehend its meaning. Think about it as you go to sleep. Think about it if you wake up briefly in the middle of the night. Think about it when you wake up in the morning. Think about it when you shower. Think about it during coffee breaks, while you drive, while you cook, while the computer is booting up, while you're in the parking lot waiting for the kids to get out of school. The more you think about it the more it'll become a part of you.

Like anything else, you will only get out of something what you put into it. If a person wants to be a professional symphonic musician it takes a lifetime of practice with their instrument. Years ago I heard or read a story about a virtuoso violinist who performed an amazing recital. After the concert a man in the audience shook the hand of the violinist and said, *"I'd give my whole life to play the violin like you do."* The violinist simply replied, *"I did."* Likewise, if we want to be successful in faith it takes a lifetime commitment on our part.

Over and over the scriptures state that the just shall live by faith:

...the just shall LIVE BY HIS FAITH.
- Habakkuk 2:4

...as it is written, The just shall LIVE BY FAITH.
- Romans 1:17

...for, The just shall LIVE BY FAITH.
- Galatians 3:11

Now the just shall LIVE BY FAITH...
- Hebrews 10:38

Some people have the attitude that faith is something that they'll try for a couple of weeks and if it doesn't pan out they'll drop it and try something else. But the phrase, *"to live by faith, "*reveals that faith is a *lifestyle*. It's a 24-hours-a-day-365-days-a-year way of life. The person who will live it will eventually rise to the top of every circumstance in life. When they first begin there will, no doubt, be a learning curve, so to speak, a renewing of the mind. Some catch on quicker than others, but the good news is, we can all catch it. Overcome any frustrations by more study of God's Word. Overcome any setbacks by more scriptural meditation. This is the victory that overcometh the world, even our faith. (1 John 5:4)

To be real honest about it, once you get hold of it you'll realize it's the easiest thing that you've ever done in your life. You'll almost shake your head back and forth in embarrassment that it ever seemed so difficult to you. You'll enter into

198

a joy that you never knew existed. *"Ask, and ye shall receive, that your JOY may be full"* (John 16:24).

NOTES